Executive Smarts

25 QUICK READS ON MANAGING FOR RESULTS

William W. Casey, Ph.D.
Wendi Peck

Executive Smarts
25 Quick Tips on Managing for Results

ISBN: 978-0-9912689-3-1

Executive Leadership Group, Inc.
Office 720-963-9212
FAX 720-963-9213
Email Info@ELG.net
Web www.elg.net

Executive Smarts is also available in an e-book format. If you enjoyed this book and would like to share it with friends or colleagues, selected content is available at:
www.ExecutiveSmartsBook.com/share

CONTENTS

3 PROJECTS AND INITIATIVES

4 ORGANIZATIONAL CULTURE AND CHANGE

If you liked these chapters and want to forward one to a friend or colleague, you may do so at:

www.ExecutiveSmartsBook.com/share

PREFACE

Each chapter of this book is aimed at quickly conveying something useful to leaders at all levels. The head of one large military organization tells us he likes our writing because we get to the point and don't waste his time. A venture capitalist says the same thing. We'll try to do the same for you.

Consider the table of contents your dim sum menu. Any sequence of chapters, in any combination, will work. This isn't the kind of book that requires you to slog your way through material that doesn't interest you to get to what does. And most chapters take no more than five minutes to read.

But please don't take the brevity and simplicity as light treatment of serious issues. Blaise Pascal famously told three bishops that he would have written them a shorter letter but he didn't have the time. Well, we took the time. So we hope you'll find the ideas and information here simple, but not simplistic; we also hope you'll find them immediately actionable, yet possessing strategic heft.

We selected our topics based on nitty-gritty issues we've seen repeatedly over the years and across many industries and sectors. Often, they are our reaction to irksome organizational patterns, such as assigning accountability without authority, or leaders who leave messes behind when they vacate a position, or project managers who cannot, themselves, be managed. Most of the ideas are applicable to organizations of all sizes.

— *William Casey*
Wendi Peck

1 LEADERSHIP AND PERSONAL EFFECTIVENESS

Leadership Transition: Leave Your Campsite Better Than You Found It

Here in Colorado, we are an outdoorsy bunch. Even those of us who prefer a hot toddy to a warm tent allow ourselves to be dragged off to the Great Wilderness now and then. With this tradition comes a farsighted ethic that you must always leave your campsite better than you found it. It's a great rule.

More executives need to learn this simple morality, because leadership transition is fraught with folks who leave a mess behind. C-level/flag-level transition, in particular, can have an aspect of political pragmatism with stinky debris trailing behind. We estimate that the ethical hierarchy sorts out along these lines:

1 (Heinous) *Close off the next leader's options.*
Only outrageous pride can account for executives who use their policy, budget, and personnel decisions to explicitly cut off the strategic options of the person who follows them. Are they really so brilliant that the next guy shouldn't have options? The sin of hubris is at the root of this ethical break.

2 (Slimy) *Leave the next leader a mess.*
A slimy transitioning leader feigns good performance by pushing problems into the future. This person saddles his or her successor with deferred maintenance (literally and metaphorically), including unattended staff problems, underinvestment in marketing and R&D, stupid staff cuts, and so on. This ethical break is essentially a con job.

3. (Out to lunch) *Ignore the issue altogether.* "Out-to-lunch" departing leaders simply aren't thinking about the next leader. Like the nearsighted cartoon character Mister Magoo, their wake of chaos is completely unintentional.
4. (Good campers) *Give the next leader the ability to steer.* A leader who is a good camper does the hard things that need doing. They fire people who need firing, fix things that need fixing, create both structure and processes for getting things done, and leave behind more than a short-term focus.

No one is perfect, and there is always plenty of work left for the next leader, but good campers distinguish themselves from others by leaving behind an organization that is more capable than when they came on board. These are the folks who are thinking about the legacy they will leave to their organization, to their employees, to their customers, and to the next leader. Kudos to those who lead with this long view.

Slow Courage and Doing the Right Thing

Why do some bureaucracies succeed while many others fail? There are endless explanations for this and we will add one more: slow courage.

We're not talking about the kind of heroism displayed in 1987 by U.S. sailor Wayne Weaver, who escaped a fierce on-board fire only to turn around and go back for his buddies — three times. On his fourth descent into the hellish flames, he did not return.

That's raw, gritty courage, the kind that brings tears to our eyes. But there is a different kind of courage. This is what keeps the wheels of the world moving, even if its practitioners don't get written up in their hometown newspapers.

People with slow courage do the right thing in organizations that reward the wrong thing. They rise above the systems they inhabit. Instead of standing as single acts of brazen bravery, theirs are heroic habits over time.

Here is the problem with most bureaucracies, public or private: They say they are out to achieve some virtuous Right Thing ("help the kids," "defend the country," "delight customers," etc.), but what they reward is realism.

Realism is about leaders who ignore maintenance of critical equipment to make their budgets look great. Realism is about taking credit for subordinates' work instead of showcasing them. Realism is about cutting everyone's budget the same percentage — the salami slice — because intelligent, surgical cuts require thought, work, and a thick hide.

On the other hand, people with slow courage are patient idealists. They say, "To hell with realism. I joined to do the Right Thing." They are the purchasing agent who buys what her company needs, not what her boss's buddies are selling; the safety inspector who digs deep enough to actually protect people, even if it annoys them; and the Pentagon cost estimator who estimates real costs rather than the "right answers" her superiors actually want.

These moral choices occur repeatedly over time. And there are no medals for making these right choices again and again. People with slow courage are not always happy people, but every day they can look at themselves in the mirror and know that they have done the right thing. It is their integrity that drives the organization to actually deliver on its promised results, if only a little at a time.

If the people with slow courage happen to be leaders, they act as the crap umbrella for their people. They shield their people, saying, "We claim to be here to do the right thing. As long as you work for me, that's what you really do. I'll protect you from the idiots; now go and do the right thing." And then they create a culture where the right thing is rewarded and the dumb thing is not. When necessary, they take the flak. Along the way, they create an island of sanity in a sea of silliness.

Anyway, this is a paean to the many, many anonymous people with slow courage. Whether you fulfill orders in a warehouse, deliver mail, or defend the country, we thank you. You don't face one great moment of truth, but many small ones. Thank you. You do the right thing. Thank you.

How to Take Charge

It's tough being the new kid on the block. It's even tougher being the new kid in charge. Yet as the tenures of executive positions become ever shorter, more leaders are finding themselves in this position as they take over from others who have moved on. Many of these new executives are not successful.

Fortunately, there are simple steps that will up the odds of success. First, before even stepping into the job, do your homework. Every organization has issues, opportunities, heroes, history, and fears. And so does the field in which the organization resides. Whether it's hedge funds or hedge trimmers, they all have their stories. If you are coming from outside the organization—or even outside the field—you have some reading to do. Once you've done your research, consider these twelve tips for taking charge in your new position.

1 *Clarify expectations.*

   Learn the goals of senior management and the organization's norms, culture, and history. Most important, clarify the expectations of those you work for. What's the home run they're hoping you'll hit? (You may have to infer what's considered "success" and then test it on your boss. Senior leaders aren't always good at discussing goals until they have a few straw men to respond to.)

2 *Learn from your predecessor.*

What were your predecessor's strategies and priorities? If possible, meet with that person. It will be easier to orient yourself to the responsibilities and expectations of your new position if you know the standard to which you will be compared.

3 *Develop good working relationships.*

Research shows that, when new executives fail, they usually have poor working relationships with two or more subordinates or with their superiors. These poor relationships tend to drive the eventually fatal poor performance, not the other way around.

For some people, the very thing that got them promoted to an executive position was their heads-down, get-the-work-done attitude. But in more senior positions, the relationships are at least as important as the work.

4 *Listen well.*

Effective relationships begin with really paying attention — a lot of attention — to what others have to say. This approach reduces fear, builds trust, and makes the listener more knowledgeable about the situation. Meet with key stakeholders — the people you will deal with regularly who can make or break you. In a large organization, an executive's stakeholders can easily number twenty or more individuals, including peers and senior management. If it is a customer-facing position, then also talk with some key customers.

5 *Meet the team.*

Get acquainted with each subordinate individually — especially during your few first weeks on the job — to familiarize yourself with their skills, desires, and fears. Find out what they think is expected of them and ask them what they think would make the organization more successful. Take notes. Though this is not the same as directly giving them a vote, taking the time to meet with subordinates one-on-one will communicate to them that you take them seriously and value their opinions.

Do more asking than telling in these meetings, but also share your background and your general goals for the organization. At this point, it is best to soft-pedal your views; do not be too specific too early, but do be aware that everyone will be eager to learn about you and your expectations. Being overly reserved will foster distrust.

6 *Do what you say.*

Ensure that even your slightest actions support your words, because employees will read great meaning into minor gestures, especially at first. An offhand joke about stupid customers could cripple your "customers-first" imperative, while staying late to help fill a customer's order could do the opposite. Show integrity to build credibility with your employees, which you will need in order to lead them effectively.

7 *Align to goals.*

To establish yourself as a successful new leader, clearly explain and align performance expectations. Clarity comes from measurable, outcome-oriented goals for yourself and each member of your team. So, avoid ambiguous and lengthy lists of activities, which clarify little and stifle creativity. Alignment comes from group discussions — rather than from one-on-one conversations — that help to establish what you need from your direct reports, what they need from each other, and how the team functions as a whole.

8 *Get support from above.*

Get support from above by demonstrating that you are supporting your boss. Demonstrate that you are supporting her agenda and check in with her frequently enough that she knows you are working on her behalf. The trust you build through these efforts will provide a runway for your own agenda to take flight.

9 *Align rewards to goals.*

Align rewards with new goals by recognizing and rewarding achievements that support your goals and administering swift correction for efforts that do not. If your organization has a decent performance management system, integrate your expectations with it to ensure that your direct reports will work to achieve the goals you have set.

10 *Honor the past.*

Recognize and respect previous policies and those who established them. Even if you do not approve of past organizational decisions, avoid badmouthing them even when you are arguing for change. You cannot engender loyalty by telling people they have been doing everything wrong (even if that is the case).

11 *Learn first, change second, repeat.*

Expect to make your mark on the organization in a two-step dance of learning, then leading change. The first iteration will take a month or two of rapid fact-finding and analysis followed by obvious and urgent fixes. The second iteration of learning and changing could take a couple of years. If you stick around long enough, you may get one or two more whacks at it before you go.

12 *Involve your subordinates in solutions.*

Don't be a lone wolf. New executives who tackle big problems alone tend to fail. After any initial triage, be sure to involve groups in assessing and diagnosing problems, either by using already recurring meetings or by forming special task forces. The analysis will be more thorough and the resulting commitment to change will be higher if your lieutenants are involved from the beginning with the problems that require their attention. Part of your job is to help your subordinates become leaders themselves; you will never do that if you route around them for the sake of expediency.

Being the new kid in charge isn't easy, but its worst pitfalls are easy to avoid. Moreover, in today's world of increasingly high executive turnover, you may find yourself with plenty of opportunities to practice the skill set required to master the "new boss" business.

The Formula for Good Judgment (and the Cure for Bad Judgment)

Fancy decision-making models abound in the world of work, but they are not what most leaders use day-to-day or meeting-to-meeting. Decision making in the business environment is based on human judgment. Not surprisingly, good judgment equals good decision making and bad judgment equals bad decision making. Fortunately, good judgment is learnable.

But first, let's explore the concept of "bad judgment," because therein lies the path to good judgment. Think about the times you've accused someone of outrageously "bad judgment." Odds are the situation fell into one of these two, opposing categories.

1 *Missing the bigger point.*

   You know the aphorism about seeing the forest for the trees. That represents one kind of bad judgment, being so focused on the details that larger issues are lost.

   Old joke alert: You've probably heard the one about the three tourists captured by cannibals in French New Guinea. To kill the tourists, the cannibals set up a guillotine abandoned by French colonialists. Tearful and shaking, the first tourist got on his knees as his head was forced into the guillotine. The blade was released and shot down the length of the guillotine, only to stop a few millimeters from the tourist's neck. The cannibals took this as a sign from above that the man was to be released, and so he was. The second tourist—well, let's cut to the chase, the same thing happened to him. As the third tourist, an engineer, got on his knees, his trained eyes squinted up at the mechanism. A smile washed over his face and he beamed at the cannibal leader, "Hey, Chief ! I think I know your problem!"

Sorry.

But we see this deadly dumb focus on details all the time. We see military briefers who will doggedly plod through each and every PowerPoint slide, regardless of the interests or needs of the audience. We see software writers who are determined to add just one more feature, until a market window slams shut. The list goes on and on. The devil is in the details indeed—and sometimes, so is the difference between success and failure.

2 *Missing the finer points.*

There is an opposite problem. Although it's not a standard aphorism, there are people who can't see the trees for the forest. You might get the occasional big, broad idea from them, but it will reflect no understanding of what is required to achieve the idea. And we've all seen the imperious executive spouting The Big Directive, clueless about what balls will be dropped, or other repercussions incurred in pursuit of this shiny new object, or as a result of it.

The nineteenth-century economist Frédéric Bastiat used this idea in distinguishing between bad economists and good economists:

"There is only one difference between a bad economist and a good one: the bad economist confines himself to the visible effect; the good economist takes into account both the effect that can be seen and those effects that must be foreseen."

THE FORMULA FOR GOOD JUDGMENT

Both kinds of bad judgment beget bad side effects. What's the cure for either type of bad judgment? Combine them. Fuse the two kinds of bad judgment together and you get good judgment. Kind of like sodium and chloride. Separately, they're toxic. Together, they're salt.

If you want to develop good judgment (or help someone else achieve it), learn to do both kinds of judgment, starting with your preferred style, and then consciously and deliberately, looping over to the other style and back again a few times. That's it.

So, if you're a tree-type person (the engineer at the guillotine), go ahead and focus on your critical details, but then loop back the other way. Give meaning and context to the details by asking questions such as these:

- What's the ultimate point here? And, what's the point of that?
- What were we originally funded to produce?
- What's the broader impact of the decision I'm considering? Could anything negative be created by my positive intentions?

Then loop back over to "crucial details" and see if you still like the game plan or want to alter it a bit. Make a couple of little-picture/big-picture loops until you are satisfied with your thinking.

That's how good judgment works: You dance from side to side, like the Texas two-step.

On the other hand, if you're a forest-type person, a Big Thinker, go ahead and revel in that Big Picture, but then loop over to Detail Land with questions such as:

- What would be the first, concrete step?
- What will it take to make this happen in terms of time, money, and effort?
- What might we have to stop doing in order to do this thing?
- Who else, or what else, might I affect with this effort?

After you've got some of those grimy details in hand, loop back to your lofty heights and see if you still like the scenery. Again — consciously and deliberately — jog around this track a few times. It is the only way to move from a vaporous vision to an actionable one, one you'll be proud of when it's achieved.

Whether you're a big-picture or a detail-oriented type, if you make the loop enough times, in the end you'll be able to see the forest and the trees. One direction will feel natural to you, but the other you will have to push yourself toward consciously and deliberately. With practice, good decision making will become habit.

ACKNOWLEDGMENT

It would be lousy judgment if we didn't credit the smart guy who came up with this model. Years ago, our friend and former colleague (and intercultural communication overlord) Dr. Milton Bennett delivered these fine thoughts in a class we were co-teaching. It made loads of sense and has stuck with us since.

How Not to Derail Your Climb Up the Corporation's Ladder

A promising executive career can be derailed many different ways. Just ask former Enron CFO Andrew Fastow. Most of those ways, however, don't involve jail time.

Scientists have researched the boneheaded things executives do to stall or end their careers, and the list is long. But the dominant career-killing theme for new executives is leaning too heavily on what worked before. It's a sad irony that the very strengths that ushered someone into the executive suite can boot him right out again.

Here are the most popular variations on that theme:

- "I'm a hands-on kind of person." That approach can work for managers determined to get the right results, even if they have to do the work themselves. But executives can't afford to be too hands-on. Executives who do all the important work instead of delegating it probably aren't building and leading their teams, which is a classic derailer. And an executive can't execute without a well-functioning team.

  Another hands-on problem is the engineer who wants to keep on engineering, or the doctor who wants to keep on doctoring — all at a higher salary, of course. Likewise, viewing all problems through the lens of their own specialty derails some executives. Regrettably, the farther up the ranks you go, the farther you get from the field you love. If you can't handle that, don't scale the ranks.

- Related to the hands-on problem is over-reliance on a single subordinate. Maybe that one person is wonderful, but why aren't his peers wonderful, too? Whose fault is that? Again, the sin is failing to create an effective team.
- "I'm too busy to play politics." Right. Head down and nose to the grindstone works lower down in the organization. But unfortunately, getting along with people (playing politics) is a job requirement as you rise up the ranks. One study cited "poor working relationships" as a factor in more than 50 percent of derailed careers. And that's not just with the boss, as we've said. It's with peers, too.

  For example, people who lead major initiatives and programs after having been promoted from lowly "project manager" are often surprised and resentful at the amount of time they have to spend schmoozing. But the ones who accept and master this transition succeed. The others get kicked back downstairs, if they're lucky.
- "I know what I'm doing." Confidence is a wonderful thing and we should all have more of it. Executives on the way up generally have plenty of it. But here's the rub: Confidence can make you stupid. It can prevent and deflect feedback that would help you get wise to the ways of "mahogany row," a culture unto itself. No amount of confidence will overcome ignorance about cultural differences. A little humility

and openness to feedback are a dandy stop-gaffe measure.

- "I'm the boss of you." There's some evidence that a heavy hand can work for managers at lower levels of the organization — though we're not advocating it — but for executives it's a grave liability and a major contributor to executive derailment.

  There are two exceptions to this rule. First, fist pounders can succeed if the organization's top executives model a similar style. But the authoritarian executive had better be prepared to switch fast when leadership changes.

  Second, bullying can work well in some turnaround situations when there just isn't any time for consensus building. The trap: This style can work so well that the executive keeps on breathing fire even when the organization is out of the woods. Even after the bully is gone, it will take years to heal the fearful organization she left in her wake.

- "I'm in over my head." A frequently given reason for executive derailment is the simple inability to handle the strategic requirements of the job.

  A seventeen-year study at the U.S. Army Research Institute in Arlington, Virginia, showed that one's ability to think strategically — one's "cognitive capacity" — derives from cognitive maturation, not training. More important, different people have different cognitive maturation curves.

> Executives who simply aren't able to think in large enough chunks are hard to help. They'll find no salvation in training, business books, coaches, or consultants. None of it will solve the essential problem.
>
> Believe us, we've seen people try. It's no picnic for these poor souls; they feel like frauds and drown their sorrows in details. Their best option is a graceful but hasty retreat to a different position, one that poses more achievable challenges.

This last, unfortunate derailer aside, the formula for executives on their way up is simple: Victory will come to you if you don't let previous successes make you inflexible.

2 PLANNING AND EXECUTION

Are Goals Dangerous?

"Goals are dangerous." So a recent spate of management literature would have you believe. Some authors argue that goals cause narrow and short-term focus, inept performance, and harmful side effects such as unethical behavior.

Say it isn't so!

Okay, we will. Goals are not dangerous. However, unstrategic and incomplete thinking, when spelling out our aims, can be disastrous. We will return to that idea, but first, let's examine the beef against goals.

THE INDICTMENT OF GOALS

Pundits who denounce goals cite anecdotes that, at first glance, seem to support their case. Here's an example:

> The Enron debacle. This case involved nefarious executives with stiff revenue goals and whopping rewards for meeting them. Unfortunately, those same goals pushed them to cook the books and drive the company into the ground.

Generally, the gripe against goals can be grouped into three categories:

1 Goals trigger sins of commission, such as taking imprudent risks, gaming the system, or overlooking side effects that harm bystanders in either the present or the future.

2 Goals trigger sins of omission, such as neglected opportunities to achieve different and better outcomes, or chances to help teammates and thereby create bigger successes.

3 Goals hurt the goal-seeker. This can happen in two ways. First, they can demotivate people who fall short of goal achievement; people who fail at a goal can become discouraged and perform even worse than they would have with no goal. Second, goals can actually hurt performance by distracting people from first learning how to do something before attempting some sort of quota or target.

These all sound like reasonable criticisms of goals, and you don't have to reach far to find examples of each kind of problem. But there are plenty of counterexamples, too.

Consider technological advances achieved when goals (and prizes!) have been established by organizations such as the X Prize Foundation and the Defense Advanced Research Projects Agency. Venture philanthropies such as the Bill and Melinda Gates Foundation credit much of their considerable success to clear, outcome-oriented goals. The prolific Thomas Edison set a goal to invent the light bulb, among many other such targets. Goals do not seem to have hurt him. In fact, goals seem to be the not-so-secret ingredient in plenty of spectacular successes.

So, we would counter the goals-are-dangerous position with this: Criticizing goals, as such, is rather like criticizing all things on television or any presentation in PowerPoint. Content matters at least as much as the container; the medium isn't always the message. Maybe, instead of debating whether goals are dangerous, we need to ask, "What kind of content makes goals safe and effective?"

CONTENT PRECEDES FORM

Much literature on goals focuses on form (e.g., "start with a verb"), but not nearly enough prescribes the strategic thinking that must happen before worrying about form. Just as it's possible for a poem with good meter and rhyme to make no sense, it's possible for a goal to be well constructed but ill considered.

As Peter Drucker remarked on the goal-based system called "management by objectives," "It works if you first think through your objectives. Ninety percent of the time, you haven't." Perhaps there is such a thing as a DUMB goal.

AIMING FOR RESULTS

Strategic thinking focuses first on what is to be achieved before it focuses on methods or steps. So the goals we're concerned with here are about results, not effort. They're about "Lose ten pounds," not "Put my fork down between bites."

In fact, many efforts fail because no end state, outcome, or result was defined at the outset. Furthermore, many declared "successes" are based wholly on how much time, effort, or money was spent on work, without even a mention of actual results. We're thinking here of, for instance, government agencies that proudly proclaim how many dollars they've spent and how many programs they've launched. Similarly, we think of corporate "quality czars" whose success seems solely expressed in terms of how many people have been trained.

IBM — a truly great company — years ago learned this lesson the hard way by setting goals and rewards based on how many lines of code its programmers wrote. The result was loads more code than needed. Now, their managers specify what the code needs to accomplish and encourage the programmers to exercise their ingenuity toward those ends.

All of us have thought, "I wish my boss would just tell me what to do and then get out of my way." But most of us weren't yearning for detailed to-dos. We were looking for a description of what needs to be accomplished and then a little leeway to achieve it. Telling knowledgeable people how to do something they can figure out on their own corrodes self-esteem and creativity.

The front end of any effort, initiative, or strategy is not the time to ask, "What should we do?" or "What's the right metric?" But it is the right time to ask, "What's the result we're looking for?" Those other questions must wait until you know what you're trying to achieve.

Admittedly, it's a cliché to recommend that goals be results-oriented. So here's the bigger question: What is it about a goal that reflects superior strategic thinking?

We've observed that the best thinkers — either explicitly or implicitly — target results that reflect three principles, and with an order in thinking that proceeds in this sequence:

- Meaningful results — reflective of sufficiently broad context.
- Restricted results — reflective of "peripheral vision" that is alert to collateral damage.
- Indisputable results — reflective of hard-nosed empiricism.

MRI: THREE PRINCIPLES TO TARGET RESULTS THAT MATTER

1 *Meaningful results.*

If you don't pause to think deeply about what you are trying to achieve, then it's easy to reach for the obvious (usually short-term) outcome instead of one that considers the bigger picture.

Insightful or clever results usually stem from larger context: The longer-term impact or the broader impact. The question to answer is, "What is really the point here?"

For example, if you have assigned a new employee to complete a project, you may be so inclined to "help" him with it such that he receives little experience while involved with it. If that happens, then you'll achieve the near-term goal of quick and perfect project completion — and miss the longer-term goal of on-boarding the new recruit. Which is the more important point?

Furthermore, the goal that considers larger context often lends more meaning to employees' work and is therefore a more powerful motivator. Telling employees, "We're here to help make sure people don't get hurt," builds a lot more fire in the belly than telling them, "We do safety inspections." Employees want to be part of something greater than themselves, and often they already are. The right goal can help them see this picture, but the wrong goal can trivialize the noblest efforts.

Had those Enron executives had a profitability goal instead of a revenue goal, they would have been closer to aiming at a "right result." (We would add the proviso that sales from one subsidiary to another, and back again, don't count as "profit.")

For example, a Canadian mental health clinic that one of our colleagues worked with changed the wording of their goal from the ambiguous platitude "to help our patients" to the more specific and inspiring aspiration "to enable our patients to live in the community." This significant shift in thinking about the clinic's goal had a huge impact on how all those in the enterprise approached their work.

Sometimes the "right result" is not better performance but simply learning how to achieve better performance. For example, in our line of work, we are often asked to help fix organizational issues. This really entails two separate projects: (1) figuring out what's causing the problem and then (2) solving the problem based on what we've learned.

It is impossible to know the content of the second project until the first one is done. While most of our clients know that this approach is common for outside consultants, people inside organizations often receive only a single goal to improve something without first getting a goal to figure out how and why that something needs to be improved.

Academics call this sort of goal a "learning goal." Research shows that these learning goals need to precede "performance goals" to facilitate good performance on a previously unknown task.

Bigger contexts can lead to a better goals. "Sometimes it's better to climb up than to drill down," as one smart client of ours commented.

2 *Restricted results.*

When goals seem to backfire, it's often because the way they were achieved wasn't appropriate. For example, you might insist that the son you are putting through college must achieve a 3.5 grade point average — and then he follows through, achieving exactly that. But he does it by taking a string of easy-A courses that won't move him much toward graduation, which isn't the way you wanted him to achieve that target.

Or an organization might set and achieve a goal to cut operating costs, as the U.S. Navy did with its ships in the early 2000s. But if savings come from cuts in training and maintenance, then a much bigger problem has been created over time than was solved, as the Navy has discovered. The way you achieve a goal matters.

Thus it is that unintended consequences can arise from the way a goal is pursued. But they can also occur another way: Unintended consequences can result from the outcome itself. As in a game of pool, you have to ask yourself, "Will I be where I want to be after I make this shot?"

For example, a company might set and achieve a goal to get all their project managers certified in project management. In general, that's a great idea; companies with certified project managers win more contracts, if that's the business they're in. And, the training will probably help them succeed with other projects as well. But one consequence of getting project managers certified is that they can now more easily move to higher paying jobs elsewhere, which many of them do. Oops.

Military people call these ripple effects "second- and third- order effects," and it is something they look out for, not always successfully. For example, the U.S.-led surprise invasion of Iraq in 2003 achieved a swift and decisive victory. Unfortunately the leaders' definition of "victory" was soon to be regretted, and for a long time.

What to do? All of this comes under the heading of "be careful what you wish for." Sometimes it helps to ask, "What could go wrong?" — and then listen to the answer. Although there is no crystal ball that will reveal all the ripple effects of your action (or inaction, for that matter), many potential bad side effects are obvious when looked for in advance. A goal that does not explicitly proscribe predictable negative side effects is simply not a complete goal. Clearly stated: Part of the goal should be a restriction on predictable harm.

The virtue called "enlightened self-interest" is often just a matter of restricted goal pursuit. For example, entrepreneurs pursue profit, politicians pursue power, and military careerists pursue advancement. We fully — and sometimes happily — expect that. But we shake our heads in wonder at the individuals who pursue these things with no thought of collateral damage or long-term effects. There is a moral dimension here.

Let's now return to that Canadian mental health clinic. Did their goal have restrictions? Yes. Aside from targeting a meaningful result, they also spelled out their restrictions.

Because they were trying to get their patients to spend more of their time in the community (and out of the hospital), they imposed this restriction: "no change in admission or discharge standards." This restriction prevented any overzealous psychologists from gaming the system, which could include throttling down the number of patient admissions, or discharging only the very few, least risky patients.

But the point is not only to target a *whole goal* — that's our term for stating the result you want plus the side-effects you don't. You also need to make exceedingly clear what success looks like, which is our next point.

3 *Indisputable results.*

A goal needs to be stated so that its achievement or nonachievement is empirically verifiable. In other words, everybody involved needs to be able to gauge whether a home run has happened. The ambiguity (and associated risk of misinterpretation) of "I'll know it when I see it" breeds frustration and waste.

Smart leaders state precisely what outcomes they're aiming for, especially when the effort can cost others' time, money, or even lives. How the goal is achieved (i.e., strategies and tactics for reaching it) might need to adjust along the way, but a well-considered outcome usually remains constant.

A couple of years ago, we were hired to help a senior military team get on the same page — "alignment and focus" is the management jargon for what they wanted. Initially, we surveyed each team member's interpretation of the organization's top-level "goals." Among nine people on a senior team, there were between three and seven radically different interpretations of each of these goals. In fact, in the case of one goal, we discovered that three different departments had launched initiatives in support of the perceived aim — all going in different directions.

Of course, fuzzy goals do have their appeal — apart from the fact that they are intellectually undemanding as well as impossible to link to accountability. They are also politically attractive; agreement comes easily when a goal is open to interpretation.

One former client, an oil executive, complained about this political convenience, saying, "Lawmakers get to take credit for the good intentions of broadly written laws, and then regulators and courts are left to interpret the mess. More specific laws would lead to better compliance, but that's hard and it's not what wins votes."

So, some leaders may benefit from imprecision, deliberate or otherwise. But anyone else — anyone actually concerned with execution — will not benefit. The arguments and rancor postponed by vague goals at the outset of an effort inevitably erupt later as squandered time, money, and trust become evident.

Getting back to that mental health center, after they expanded their goal to make it whole — right result plus restrictions — then they made it indisputable. Here was the wording: "Increase the number of days between patient discharge and re-admission by at least 50%, with no change in admission or discharge standards." This was a target they hit.

Of course, it's nice to know whether you've succeeded, which clear goals help you do. But, almost as important, clear goals will help you know whether you've failed. If you've got a flop on your hands, at least it ought to be an instructive one. Fuzzy flops mean you've paid your tuition but didn't go to school.

If you can't say clearly what you had hoped for, it will be hard for experience to teach you what works and what doesn't. For example, if I kick a football into an open field with no clear target, then my effort will result in neither success nor failure. Who can say whether I'm getting better or worse if I don't know what success looks like? Merely spending time and money with no clear sense of a desired outcome is not even "experimenting," it is merely dabbling, and it begets little learning or innovation.

SUMMING UP

So, are goals dangerous? Sure, kind of like fire, electricity, mighty rivers, teenage daughters, and many other forces of nature. But there are known principles for harnessing these forces (except maybe teenage daughters) — principles that require strategic thinking. The trick with goals is to aim for meaningful results, enlist boundaries with a few well-considered restrictions, and then state them indisputably.

A Clear Success? You Bet!

Any serious strategist must ask, "How will we know when we've succeeded?" Strategies have intended outcomes — goals — and it's critically helpful if those outcomes are clear enough that success or failure will be indisputable.

Here we are offering an alternative to the usual questions, such as "Do we have metrics?" or worse, "Do we have enough metrics?" Instead, lead with, "Is success defined so clearly that we could place a bet on it?"

THE BAR BET

At some point most of us have been in good-natured arguments with friends that amounted to not much more than redundant bickering. Such as:

You (beer in hand): "Yeah, I've seen that guy play. He's a natural-born athlete. He's going to have a great first year."

Friend: "I doubt it. He might have natural talent, but he hasn't developed it yet. I predict a ragged first year for that guy."

You: "No way! He's going to surprise everyone. That guy is good."

Friend: "You're crazy."

And so on. But then something magical happens, something wonderful, something that halts the bickering and utterly elevates the conversation: One of you says, "I'll bet you twenty bucks that you're wrong."

This is the kind of comment that, as some academics would say, provokes an "epistemological shift." Now you both must work together to agree on objective and verifiable proof of success — a definition of "a great first year."

If you have ever been through this kind of bar chatter, then you know exactly how to have "the right metrics." It's all about crafting such a clear description of success that you and a friendly skeptic can bet on it. It's that simple.

NONBETABLE vs. BETABLE

Some typically vague (nonbetable) strategic goals, and some bet-able alternatives:

You couldn't bet on (or against) these:	*But you could bet on (or against) these:*
We're going to build a culture of safety.	We're going to reduce worker days lost due to injuries on or off the job by at least 50 percent.
We'll become more energy conscious.	We will achieve at least a 20 percent month-to-month reduction in kilowatt hours per square meter of building space over the previous twelve months.
We'll raise public awareness of our organization.	In this calendar year, there will be at least ten articles that mention our name in the *Wall Street Journal* and/or the *New York Times.*

The left-hand column, the nonbetable goals, are where most of us start our thinking, which is fine. It's natural to consider general direction before targeting specific results. The problem is when we content ourselves with general direction only, and stop short of a bettable goal. That's when we deny ourselves and our teammates the benefit of an unambiguous bulls-eye.

GO AHEAD AND ARGUE

Notice that you might not agree with all our betable alternatives. That's a good thing. It means the proposed definition of success is so clear that we can argue over it before we start spending time and money to achieve it!

Next time you make a grand declaration of direction ("We're going to be an employer of choice," or, "We're going to provide humanitarian assistance," or "I'm going to start being a better parent," for example) ask yourself how you would define success if someone bet twenty dollars against you. If your declaration passes the "bar bet" test, then you're good to go. The people paying for the result will know what they're getting, the people doing the work will have clear direction, and you will have the satisfaction of knowing — without question — whether you're successful.

Strategic Assumptions – A Prerequisite to Great Strategies

Strategic plans almost always assume certain things to be true about the future. For example, when one company plans to acquire another, its leaders may assume they can achieve synergies to drive down costs. They might assume they are buying their way into a high-growth market or blocking a competitor's moves. Or they could assume a combination of the above.

Unfortunately, many strategic plans include assumptions that don't mean much. And some plans just skip the idea altogether: Lousy or absent assumptions cause problems, such as:

- Strategy is harder to get right the first time. Discussion and debate works best when our premises are crisp and defensible. Clear premises enable clear thinking. In strategic planning, assumptions are our premises, and it's hard to think clearly without good ones.
- Strategy is harder to correct quickly. Strategy should be corrected immediately when its underlying assumptions don't play out. But that's tough to do when you don't know what your assumptions are.

Strong strategy — and quick course correction — require clear and useful strategic assumptions.

Here are ten tips on how to make sure you get exactly that.

1 *Keep your head out of the sand.*

As kids, both of us (Wendi & Bill) were lectured that, "To assume makes an 'ass' of 'u' and 'me.'" This was always in reference to an assumption that hadn't been discussed until it didn't pan out — "But, Mom, I assumed somebody would give me a ride home!" That's when the lectures began.

Many strategic plans have the same problem, their important assumptions being unexpressed or obscured. If mentioned at all, they are banal, such as, "There will continue to be competition." They might as well say, "There will continue to be air." They declare the obvious without contributing anything useful.

Consequently, pivotal assumptions go unstated. We call this flaw the "head-in-the-sand" problem — obliviousness to what one is actually assuming. This is the most pernicious problem we see with assumptions and strategic plans. It is the inability or unwillingness to actually state what you are assuming.

2 *Stay above hubris.*

Hubris is another common problem. Too many plans arrogantly assume away important barriers, pitfalls, and problems. For example, when we blithely assume that a complex, technical project will come in on time and on budget, we are presuming godlike powers not normally associated with reality. When we assume that our advances will cow rather than invigorate a strong competitor, we are living on a different planet.

The point of strategic assumptions is not to sweep away problems, but instead to articulate a likely reality. Chest-thumping strategic goals are fine; chest-thumping assumptions are dangerous. They project an optimistic future or capability without provisions for achieving them.

Louis Armstrong wanted “A Kiss to Build a Dream On” (wonderful song); a strategic assumption is a guess to build a strategy on. So it had better be a pretty good guess.

3 *Really question your assumptions.*

Although it helps to be a pragmatic optimist when writing strategic goals, we suggest you play the pragmatic skeptic when writing assumptions.

The assumption-writer asks annoying questions such as, “Will the adversary truly respond the way we think he will?” “Has this ever worked in the past?” “On what basis do we think funding will continue to be available?” “How good are we, usually, at implementing big ideas?” “Why do we think our competitors’ technology will not advance sufficiently for them to gain the advantage?” “Do our constituents really want the same things they need?”

To write good assumptions, temporarily divorce yourself from your enthusiasm for the plan, platform, personality, or future. Launch a cascade of cranky questions. Call in diverse and dispassionate experts who have no vested interests in your situation and ask them periodically to “red team” your plans — with critical questioning of your unstated premises.

Get them to explicitly articulate your assumptions about what your own organization is capable of — and then question those assumptions. Get them to do the same with assumptions about your external environment, such as adversaries, allies, technology, legislation, and so on.

4 *Think of categories before you think of assumptions.*

Before you and your team (and red team) brainstorm assumptions, you will find it immensely helpful to first brainstorm categories of assumptions. Cognitive psychological research (and our experience) indicates that people will generate about twice as many useful ideas if they have categories in which to fit them. So, for example, an assumptions brainstorm for a commuter airline might start by identifying possible assumption categories such as:

- Legislation and regulation
- Interest rates
- Fuel costs
- Quality and cost of non-face-to-face meeting technology
- Labor markets
- Miscellaneous (none of the above, but relevant)

After categories have been identified, then most people will have an easier time generating assumptions. And remember always to include a "none of the above" category; the list is meant to be an aid to thinking, not a constraint.

5 *Close the assumption-strategy loop.*

In theory, you should start by generating a nice, clean

set of assumptions before crafting strategic goals. After all, good assumptions enable solid strategic goals. But the truth is, the whole process is a messy, iterative loop that can start anywhere you like. Feel free to start with glorious strategic goals and then question the assumptions that supported those goals. Or start with assumptions and build strategic goals on that foundation. In either case, circle back and forth from one to the other a few times before you settle on assumptions and strategic goals. This is like the good judgment loop we discussed in an earlier chapter ("The Formula for Good Judgment").

6 *Keep your plan relevant.*

Good implementers continually ask, "How are we doing against our plan?" Great implementers ask further, "Is our plan still relevant?" A powerful way to address relevance is with your assumptions. If your assumptions have not held true, or have been incomplete, then it's time to rethink the plan. Even before your results tell you that your plan is off the mark, occasional review of your assumptions serves as an early warning system before bad results start rolling in, and informing you that something needs changing. Here are the kinds of questions to ask:

- "Our plan assumed that corn would stay below $6 per bushel. Has it?"
- "Our plan assumed that our competitors would lower

their price at least 10 percent within six months of our entry to the market. Did they?"

- "Our plan assumed that our two Singapore plants could consolidate without a reduction in monthly output after six months. Did they?"

If you have tied strategies to assumptions, then you'll have a considerable advantage in knowing what to change when the assumptions have to change.

7 *Make them crystal-clear.*

Of course, just knowing your assumptions will put you ahead of the pack, both as a planner and as an implementer. But knowing exactly what you mean by each assumption will put you even further ahead. We have written elsewhere about the importance of clear and measurable strategic goals. Well, the same goes for assumptions.

Precision and specificity are essential, because assumptions such as, "The market for widgets will continue to grow" aren't terribly useful. Such unfocused assumptions can create confusion and disagreement. Worse, broad, fuzzy assumptions tend to be ignored and disconnected from strategic adjustments. Much better are specific assumptions such as, "The market for widgets will continue to grow at least 3% per quarter," which can be monitored as a straightforward and unambiguous task.

8 *Connect assumptions to strategies.*

There is another requisite for the correction loop to

work: The relationship of a strategic goal to one or more assumptions should be absolutely explicit. Otherwise it's too difficult to change your strategy, even if you spot mistakes in your assumptions as reality unfolds. Too often, there is no clear relationship between the strategies in a strategic plan and the assumptions on which they are based. The relationship between assumptions and strategies need not be only one assumption to one strategy. Those relationships can also be many-to-one or one-to-many.

9 *Make contingency plans.*

If assumptions are measurable, they serve as effective tripwires for contingency plans. For example, your strategic plan might state, "If assumptions x, y, and z hold true, we'll stick with course A. But if any two of them prove incorrect, we'll switch to course B." In other words, you don't need to wait until an assumption proves wrong to create a replacement strategy.

Furthermore, your contingency plan needn't always be a fallback plan. If assumptions turn out to be too conservative or pessimistic, it may be useful to also have a "seize-the-opportunity" plan.

10 *Hedge your bets.*

"Hedging" is one way to prepare for the eventuality of incorrect assumptions. A hedge is a relatively small upfront investment that can mitigate the impact of incorrect assumptions. A hedge may include the purchase of equipment that might never be needed (like a seat belt), training you probably will never need (like CPR instruction), or the right to use or lease something that might never be part of your future.

For example, in a municipality where it hardly ever snows, a savvy mayor might insist on purchasing a single snow plow or, better yet, snow plow attachments for existing trucks — and annual maintenance and training on the (probably idle) equipment.

Or one portion of a strategic plan might rest on the assumption that, "Public support for our work will continue to grow at its present pace for at least three more years." But here is the "hedge": "We will identify three specialists in handling crisis public relations, have their 24-hour contact information prepared, and meet with at least one of them."

IN SUMMARY

Well-considered assumptions make your strategic plan smart and relevant. They give you a logical foundation and an ongoing grounding in reality. And, like many things in life that are simultaneously both simple and hard, your payoff for careful attention to assumptions will many times exceed your investment.

Accomplish More with Less

We know more than a few people who are bitter about being asked to "do more with less." We understand. If you are asked to keep doing the same stuff but with less money and manpower, it feels like your only options are to work faster or longer, which after a point becomes ridiculous. We urge, instead, a stance embodied by the slogan "accomplish more with less."

One reader of *Government Executive* magazine reacted to President Obama's 2011 call for leaner government by commenting, "[Doing] 'more with less' just makes those who are left to do the work overburdened, underappreciated, and ready to call it quits!" That mood isn't confined to the public sector.

Another sentiment we've seen in spades expresses the intention to do less with less: "You cut my budget by twenty percent? Fine. I'll cut my output by twenty percent." Unfortunately, doing less with less isn't effective in today's world. Whether we work in advertising or airlines, we all have to up our game to stay in the game.

Most people who try to up their game do so by aiming for greater efficiency. It seems like the obvious place to start. But, granting that most organizations could use some streamlining, we'd suggest that anyone facing a belt-tightening consider answering these three questions first.

1 *What's the point?*

An admiral we know once remarked, "Before doing anything else, leaders have to ask the existential question: 'Why does my organization exist?'" He's right. What is the purpose or objective of your team, your organization, your project, or your process?

A mega-project in one Fortune 500 company had dragged on for a year with no discernable progress, and burning a couple of million dollars per month. Then a new executive was put in charge of the project. Her first question was: "What's the point?" After considerable probing, she learned that the point of the project was to update the company's financial systems sufficiently to enable acquisitions, a cornerstone of the new CEO's strategy (one that turned out to be right). Once the point of the work was put on the table, the project executive could then organize all the work around it, eliminate wasteful activities, and focus on the stuff that mattered, all of which she did, and with spectacular results.

Asking "what's the point?" takes us a conceptual level higher than the old "effectiveness-before-efficiency" dictum. A thoughtful answer to that question provides extraordinary leverage for anyone who wants to achieve impact. If the military strategist Carl von Clausewitz was right when he said that the essence of strategy is to concentrate one's forces on the "decisive point," then one decisive point worth knowing is the point of one's organization, regardless of its size.

2 *How will I know when I've achieved The Point?*

Pondering this question is the first step toward stating your point so clearly that you and everybody else involved will know exactly what a home run looks like.

If you can do that, you will achieve what social scientists call high "inter-observer reliability." In other words, you and your team will be able to agree whether something is actually happening rather than just hope you will know it when you see it.

For example, if a help desk department were to define their point as maximizing the productivity of their users, then they would be aimed in a good direction. At least they would know that their job is ultimately about users rather than technology. However, without a more specific goal, a lot of time and money could be ill spent in the service of "maximizing productivity."

A more specific goal might be, "Users will experience at least 99% uptime for their computers and smartphones" or "None of our users will report that their work was delayed due to technological breakdowns or outages." Such clarifications are important because these two specific goals might drive different behavior — and spending decisions — even though they are both based on "maximizing productivity."

3 *What should we stop doing because it doesn't achieve the point?*

Paradoxically, the people who whine loudest about being asked to do more with less seem to be the ones who have the hardest time letting go of work. By "letting go," we do not mean cutting back on existing effort; we mean completely stopping entire categories of activity that are not necessary or useful for reaching the primary goal. If activities don't help achieve "the point," then they are pointless.

THE PRIZE

Answering these three pointed questions nets this reward: It frees people to focus on what they need to accomplish. It makes what they are doing more meaningful because it concentrates their attention on what actually matters. And with that kind of focus, it's amazing how creative, resourceful, and energized people can be.

Yes, people can even accomplish more with less, if only they understand the point of their efforts.

When we held a "Results Roundtable" for one senior leader and his team, he cautioned us in advance that it would be a short discussion because everybody already knew the results they were there to achieve. To his surprise, it was not a short discussion, and it was not at all clear that his team understood as well as he did what they were supposed to accomplish.

Afterward, he said it was the best such session he could recall. When we asked why, he said, "Because now we're all focused on the right things and can stop doing the things that don't matter."

Exactly.

The Three C's of Accountability

"It's an accountability problem." This is one of those diagnoses that sound definitive and inspire lots of nods around the conference table. Much like "It's a leadership issue" and "It's a communication problem."

But in this case, a diagnosis is not a prescription. We believe it's just the starting point. First ask some key questions: What does "accountability" really mean? When is it present? When is it missing? Why is it missing? The answers to these questions will lead to a prescription.

In conversations and seminars with leaders over many years we developed an operational definition of accountability. This definition actually leads to a cure.

The existence of accountability requires these three elements:

1 *Clear request from an authorized manager.*

2 *Commitment from the subordinate to complete the assignment.*

3 *Consequences for performance.*

This formula sounds simple enough, but each of the elements can be difficult to deliver. Consequently, accountability can be elusive. So, here are a few thoughts on each element.

1 *Clear request from an authorized manager.*

Often, we mistake our own redundancy for glistening lucidity. Just as often, we mistake our audience's apparent agreement — or fawning — for genuine understanding.

One tech company's CEO confided to us that he wanted

to fire seven of his eight vice-presidents. He was serious. "They just don't get it," he complained, explaining that he couldn't get them all pointed in the same direction.

But he had talked to them in broad strokes and his request was not crystal clear. So we spent time with each VP, clarifying expected outcomes, until each outcome was measurable and verifiable. Performance increased dramatically and the CEO whittled his firing list down to one particular VP (a good pick).

Another reason leaders sometimes give unclear direction is that they have thought about something so much that it has come to seem intuitively obvious. To them. This is similar to what you might experience when someone frequently uses an acronym that you couldn't possibly know, or when a clerk is flummoxed that you are not familiar with a bureaucratic rule that she lives with daily.

Finally, leaders may sometimes give unclear direction because they are unclear about the destination. Their reasoning seems to be, "Let me think the big thoughts and you run along and figure out the details." However, there is a difference been tactical details and precise direction; leaders should not have to figure out all the details of execution in order to spell out precisely the desired outcome.

2 *Commitment from the subordinate to complete the assignment.*

Subordinates do not need to agree with an assignment but they do need to commit to following it. The two requisites for obtaining that commitment are (1) to provide an opportunity for dialogue and (2) to provide an explanation of why the assignment is important — give a little context.

Rare instances aside (e.g., military operations or medical emergencies), leaders can trigger the opportunity for dialogue. In its simplest form, this can be as straightforward as the closing line to an email: "Please contact me directly if you have any questions or suggestions concerning this assignment."

Dialogue generates understanding for both parties. Sometimes the authorized assigning manager becomes more informed about what he or she is requesting — or ought to be requesting — by talking with someone who actually does the work. We use these opportunities to ask questions, clarify expectations, and offer ideas. A bonus from this endeavor: It also creates mutual respect.

Dialogue often leads to a discussion of why something is being requested, which is that second requisite for commitment. Knowing the "why" gives people a context for thinking about how best to approach their assignments. Also, and perhaps more important, it gives their tasks meaning. A command to "do it because I told you to" works no better for grown-ups than for our children. Why? Because it provides no context. In fact, we believe that a leader has a moral duty to continually help his or her people see how their work fits into a bigger picture.

3 *Consequences for performance.*

Imagine that you have been in a meeting, made a clear request of one of the participants, and received earnest commitment, which was then followed by … nothing. No outcome, no performance. Maybe the problem is absence of performance consequences.

Your work likely fell into a queue behind other work on that person's plate and guess what? Your work — of lesser or no consequence — was continually displaced by other work — of greater consequence — until your work fell off the plate.

Our first element of accountability specifies that the clear request must come from an *authorized* manager. We inserted this critical word years ago at the suggestion of now-deceased management genius, Elliott Jaques. (Google him; it's worth your time.) Managers who have been duly authorized can deliver performance consequences more easily than those who have not.

Now, we hope that you don't equate the word consequence with punishment, like one of our friends who thought it sounded like we wanted to take nonperformers out back and shoot them. We don't—at least, most of the time.

Consequences can also refer to positive rewards. Positive performance consequences can range from a private statement of thanks for good performance to public praise, bonuses, promotions, and opportunities to do preferred work, while negative performance consequences can include reprimands, negative performance appraisals, and firings. Research has shown that a 4:1 ratio of specific compliments to corrections maintains an optimal work environment. (We're pretty sure there's no research on taking nonperformers out back and shooting them.)

Interestingly enough, performance consequences do not need to happen every single time to be effective; only the possibility of such consequences is necessary to create accountability.

We believe that if you find a way to apply our three C's of accountability — Clear request, Commitment, and Consequence — you will also find a cure to your organization's accountability problems.

How to Make Strategy Review = Strategy Execution

Strategy execution is about getting other people, and yourself, to do things — the right things. And that doesn't happen in the typical, annual strategic planning ritual where people throw around some ideas and then check in a year later. Like weighing yourself every morning or checking the car's fuel gauge when you get in your car, we all need to know how we're doing while there's still time to act.

One of the simplest and best tactics in the struggle to execute strategy is the "goal review meeting." In a goal review meeting the team executing a strategic plan assesses their progress against that plan. The team might be the most senior one in the organization, or it might be departmental, or anything in between, including a project team. As long as they've broken their strategy(s) into goals with individual accountability, this approach will work. (If they haven't done that — well, that would be the place to start.) For years, we've been helping our clients with these meetings, and we've learned six success factors that make them work.

1 *Include the right people.*

The people who are accountable for executing the plan are the ones who attend the goal reviews. That means the team leader — say, CEO — must be in the meeting, and so must those direct reporters who each own a portion of the plan. That's two tiers of management; don't crowd three or four tiers of management into a room. If the plan cascades down through the organization, then each subordinate team can hold its own meetings for its portion of the plan.

Sending delegates instead of the accountable parties to the meeting is generally a no-no. And if the boss can't attend, then the meeting should simply be rescheduled. These meetings require that the people who are accountable stand in front of boss and peers and describe their progress. When substitute players are sent in, the meetings lose their effect.

Staff members who can contribute should also be invited. For example, if the organization possesses a planning staff — people who look after the planning process — then members of that staff should naturally attend. In fact, they should facilitate the meetings if they have the training to do so.

If specialized topics will be discussed, then summon the specialists. For example, if legal issues will be discussed, consider inviting corporate counsel as a resource to answer questions.

2 *Meet often enough to matter.*

Most organizations we've worked with hold their strategic goal review meetings monthly, bimonthly, or quarterly (never less often than quarterly). Project goal review meetings are typically held weekly.

What's the best frequency? Meet more frequently when launching an effort because the plan is still being tested and understood. Both the people and the plan need more frequent cycles in early phases. You can throttle back a little — say, from biweekly meetings to a six-week cycle — after it's clear that everyone is up and running.

Lean toward more frequent meetings, too, if you are imposing a lot of change on your organization or if the environment is imposing a lot of changes on your organization. Think of how often you make steering adjustments when you are driving a car fast, or when the road changes frequently. Same idea.

Frequent meetings accomplish several things:

- *Focus.* They keep people focused on execution. Day-to-day distractions tempt us all hugely, so the pressure to report progress in goal review meetings keeps everyone moving ahead and aimed in the right direction.

- *Flexibility.* They keep us agile. As people get into strategy execution, opportunities and problems are revealed and the team needs to respond accordingly. For example, one team member says, "I've got three people out with the flu, so I'm at a standstill on this." Another team member says, "I can loan you a couple of my people for a week." Or the boss can say, "Outsource that piece so we can move ahead."

- *Alignment.* These meetings not only help the organization stay focused and flexible, but they also keep team members flying in formation with each other and constantly mindful of how they are affecting each other. Expressed less positively, these meetings make it much harder for one person to "succeed" at the expense of teammates.

One more related point: Schedule enough time for a meaningful on-topic discussion. Time spent productively in goal review meetings will save a multiple of that time later on. That may mean scheduling two hours and it may mean scheduling two days. When you are starting up, expect your meetings to take more time as everyone learns the routine. Later, when the team learns how to conduct these structured meetings, they will require less time.

3 *Sequence discussions around the leader's goals.*

A goal review meeting is not your standard "How's it going?" meeting, where each person in turn updates everybody else on his or her respective activities. A goal review meeting is ultimately about the leader's goals and the meeting is structured that way.

The leader has a handful of goals, the achievement of which is the point of the plan. The other team members have subordinate goals, which essentially are the plan. Discussions should be organized around the leader's goals. So, for instance, if the leader has four goals, then all subordinate goals that contribute to the leader's first goal would be briefed first, followed by discussions about goals that contribute to his second goal. And so on.

Often, a subordinate goal will contribute to more than one of the overarching goals. In that case, the goal owner should brief it at the first opportunity. One goal, for example, might contribute to larger goals #2, #3, and #4. In that case, the goal owner should brief it when goal #2 is being discussed.

4 *Use a template for the goal readouts.*

Here's another thing that will help corral a productive discussion: give the team members a briefing template to work from for each goal discussion. A good template will ensure that everyone answers the same basic set of questions about each goal and at roughly the same level of resolution. You will want the template to prompt responses to questions such as:

- What was the status of this goal last time I reported (red, yellow, or green)?
- What is it now?
- What are my key strategies for achieving this goal?
- What are my key strategies for preventing collateral damage?
- What is the "actual vs. plan" on milestones or key activities?
- What are the greatest risks (internal or external) to success?
- What are my risk mitigation strategies?
- Where do I need help from either peers or boss?*

5 *Use a facilitator to ensure productive collaboration.*

The entire team, including the leader, should be able to

* You're free to use our version of this, in PowerPoint format, at www.elg.net

focus their brainpower on the plan and its execution. The meeting process itself should be the concern of someone different: a meeting facilitator. A good one will not just waltz into the room with a flipchart and a smile. She'll work many hours before the meeting to wire it for success, will perform postsession documentation and follow-up, and will oversee the meeting process so you don't have to.

For example, you should expect a facilitator to:

- Ensure that there is cross-talk among the team members, not just a hub and spoke discussion with the boss.
- Keep track of — and post — agreements and decisions made last time, so you don't keep re-deciding the same things.
- Pull quiet members into the discussion, especially when it's obviously a topic of interest or relevance to them.

Even if you must conduct meetings by teleconference or video teleconference, it's smart to lean on skilled facilitation to help the team make the most of its time together.

6 *Reflect progress visually.*

This is going to sound like a nit, but it's not. During the meeting — as the story of your team's progress unfolds — have your facilitator or assistant build a visual display that tells the story. We like to create a large "goal map" that shows the top tier goals and their subordinate goals underneath. This can be shown electronically, but for face-to-face meetings a large paper wall chart works better. At the end of each goal status presentation, a status sticker — a red, yellow, or green dot — is placed on the chart next to the goal.

By slowly fleshing out this "you are here" map during the meeting, you show the team what they have accomplished as well as what remains to be done. This is a gentle, motivating exercise in accountability. If practical, keep this chart posted until the next meeting, where team members can see it.

IN SUMMARY

Our military clients talk metaphorically about the importance of a "drumbeat," something that keeps everyone pointed in the same direction, and moving. Consider the goal review meeting as a simple drumbeat to help you and your team move quickly, adaptively, and in alignment with one another.

3 PROJECTS AND INITIATIVES

Strategic Project Control Starts with Asking the Right Questions

If you sponsor a large organizational project, then you're supposed to know what's happening with it and with all the money it's costing. Your biggest hurdle to that task will be communication. Although some of the project managers reporting to you will make sure you know what you need to know when you need to know it, others will either swamp you with details, jolly you along with airy good news, or tell you nothing at all.

Techniques such as executive dashboards and project management office suites can help sort out the confusion. But one technique has been around since Hammurabi and it's one that all good leaders hone to a fine edge: Ask smart questions.

But problems lurk within this simple intent. Even exceptional leaders may sometimes wonder what to ask when probing for project progress. These five categories of questions may help:

1 *Project manager performance.*

Examine the performance of that person. Look for what else could be done or provided to make the project manager successful. Examples:

- What are your biggest challenges right now?
- What are your plans for dealing with those challenges?
- Is there anything I can do to make your job easier?
- (And, if things are going well) I'm glad things are going so well. If that were to change and you were to

experience a problem, from what direction do you think it might come?

2 *Project team dynamics.*

Determine if the team members are getting along, focused on the right things, and performing as needed. Examples:

- How well do your team members understand their roles and the roles of those around them?
- How well is the team working together?
- For those people who are borrowed from functional areas, are you receiving the support needed from their supervisors?
- Are there any team members who seem not to support recent team decisions?
- Do the team members have the skills they need?
- What can I do to help with the team?

3 *Project approach and outcomes.*

Learn the current results, cost, schedule and risks, and the likely trade-offs between those factors. Examples:

- Do you think our current project approach is still on target?
- Is the goal we established for this project still the correct one? Is it achievable?
- Have you made any commitments that aren't yet reflected in the current project financials?

- Are there any new changes to the project's scope that I don't know about?

4 *Earned value.*

As a project executive, you benefit from understanding a bit of project management esoterica called "earned value." In a nutshell, it takes the pulse of the project by examining budget, schedule, and work achieved — in relationship to each other rather than each as a separate concept. To get a feel for earned value, consider questions such as:

- Have we completed the work that needed to be completed by this date?
- Have we spent more or less money completing that work than we planned?

5 *Client expectations (if the client is other than you).*

Uncover current client expectations and how to manage them in the face of changing reality. And remember that "client" can mean people external to your company, or beneficiaries of your project who are inside the company. Use questions such as these:

- Do you detect any problems with the client?
- What inconsistencies are we hearing between what the executive client wants and what others in their own organization expect?
- Are you receiving enough client support from the individuals who have regular interaction with the project team?

Like the circus juggler spinning plates, you must spread your on-going attention across all five areas of inquiry. The fact that one area seems all right does not mean you can turn your back on it. Further, for each of these five areas, no single question is always the right one or the only one. The questions will change based on the project phase and circumstances.

THE POINT

Keep your eye on all five balls. With smart questions, you'll know enough to guide your project managers and your project to success.

Cross-Functional or Dysfunctional? Keys to Getting Those Big Initiatives Right

Big organizations breed cross-functional initiatives like overripe bananas breed fruit flies. And that's a good thing, because when these initiatives work, they propel an organization forward. That's because they draw from different parts of the organization — with different expertise and different interests at stake — and then focus on solving a single, important problem.

But they don't always work. In fact, a cross-functional initiative can easily become a dysfunctional one, propelling the organization nowhere. Or worse.

Here are common types of dysfunctional initiatives, plus their antidotes.

1 *Zombies.*

By definition, "initiatives" have a beginning and an end. That's because they're actually projects, a point we'll cover in the next chapter. They may last a few months or even a few years. Then they're over. But some initiatives become undead: lifeless, aimless — and endless — sucking morale and money but giving nothing back, ever.

Antidote #1: Forget to define a home run up front, and it will zombify any initiative. If no one has answered the question, "What's the point?" then the initiative is pointless — and endless. In one study we conducted, we found unclear goals to be the single biggest contributor to initiative failure.

So, before you begin planning, staffing, stakeholdering, or anything else, ask yourself, "How *exactly* will things be different if we succeed?" And don't cheat by referring to the initiative itself. For example, the point of an ERP initiative is not to install ERP software. That's circular. It will be something else. But if you can't describe success at the end, there will be neither success nor an end.

Antidote #2: Only after you have clear goals can you have clear roles, which is the other cure for zombieism. People need to know what's expected of them: What are their deliverables? With whom will they work, and on what? When do they need to kick into gear, and when should they wait on someone else?

Otherwise, everyone wanders around, confused, having the same meetings over and over again, and bumping into each other—like zombies.

2 *Unguided missiles.*

Unlike zombies, unguided missiles do actually hit a target. Unfortunately, it's the wrong target. Here's what happens.

The senior executive launching the initiative chats with the initiative's team leader. They talk in broad terms and then they go their separate ways. Afterward, the executive and the team leader don't talk much — perhaps only enough to agree that "everything is green."

Boy, are they in for a shock.

Throughout the work, the executive reflects on the initiative, staying in touch with shifting priorities. He may discuss it with peers. He does all this naturally, and it naturally refines his thinking.

Even hard-won insights soon seem plain and obvious. Meanwhile, down in Initiative Land, the team leader and his gang sink into their work and form their own ideas of what the initiative is all about, clarifying goals, roles, and tactics, which may shift as they adapt to the reality of the work.

In this scenario, mistargeted missiles are inevitable. At the end of the initiative, the only thing shared by the executive and the team is exasperation.

Antidote: The sponsoring executive and the team leader need to talk specifics. They need to agree on the verifiable point of the project (as we suggested a moment ago), and then they need to keep talking throughout the life of the initiative. Here's the surprising thing: They don't actually need to spend much time in conversation; they just need to do it often.

We like the way one savvy U.S. Navy admiral puts it: Communication early and often "ensures we don't build the perfect ladder that's leaning against the wrong wall."

3 *Cesspools.*

Many cross-functional initiatives aim to execute strategy, or otherwise accomplish things that matter to the organization. So it's always odd when managers place these weighty initiatives in the hands of lightweight team members, people who won't be missed back at their desks. What should be a talent pool isn't one. It's a cesspool of benchwarmers and neophytes.

Antidote: Obviously, the antidote here is to put the right people on the initiative. Why don't people do that? Often the problem here can be traced back to the problem we described earlier: When the "return" part of ROI is undefined, then the "investment" part is hard to swallow, especially if you're investing precious talent. First, define "the win" (sound familiar?); then it's much easier to select the best people and invest their time.

3 *Boneless chickens.*

Cartoonist Gary Larson once drew a picture of a boneless chicken ranch, with chickens draped like wet rags all over the scene. Now, reimagine those chickens as members of cross-functional initiatives — good-looking chickens all, but without a leg of authority to stand on.

Note that a cross-functional initiative is an actual organization, just like a department or a division. The fact that it is only temporary does not lessen the participants' need for ordinary authorities. In fact, it heightens the need. Lack of authority will leave them all flopping around, but getting nowhere.

Antidote: If the lead is accountable for the outcome of the initiative (she is, right?), then she needs managerial authorities commensurate with her accountability, just as though she were running a department.

Likewise, initiative team members need to be able to speak on behalf of their departments — if that's what's required of their contributions. They must not be relegated to note-taking and permission-asking.

The executive launching the initiative should openly spell out who has what authorities. People cannot self-anoint. When a peer claims, "Trust me, I'm in charge," it never works.

IN SUMMARY

Cross-functional initiatives start behind the eight ball. In most cases, they're introducing change that not everybody likes, they have no dedicated office space or administrative support, and they're filled with part-timers who may or may not support the initiative. So, give them the benefit of clear goals, clear roles, ongoing communication with senior leadership, and team members skilled and authorized to do their work.

Tips for Managing Projects More Effectively

Many managers don't know when or how to use the skill set called "project management." Even in industries where success hinges on skillful project management — construction, software development, aerospace — managers forget to use it on large initiatives aimed at their own organizations.

Whether it's an organizational restructuring or a new accounting system, any large undertaking is a project, and all projects demand the time-tested disciplines of project management. Although mastery of project management does not come easily, any manager can understand its basics.

1 *Know when you've got a project.*

Projects have a beginning, middle, and end, unlike many organizational activities. For example, installing a new performance management process is a project, running it is not. Projects involve more than one or two employees. They can have — at the least — dozens of tasks, with interdependencies among them ("We've got to do these three things before we can do that thing, but at the same time we need to be working on . . .")

One thing you can count on: Any big organizational change is a project regardless of what you call it — "initiative," "campaign," "program," or whatever.

2 *One person is in charge.*

Most co-leadership simply does not work. Just as two captains should not attempt to command a single ship, no matter how large, two project managers should not attempt to lead a single project, no matter how big or expensive. Despite any efforts to clarify the leaders' roles, the usual result of co-leadership is confusion to the team and enmity between the leaders. And whatever you do, don't put a committee in charge. Committees can advise, but not manage.

3 *Delegate authority to the person in charge.*

Accountability to produce results through others — without the authority to get those results — has derailed many hapless project managers. Finagle a way to give project managers some semblance of the four basic authorities any other manager has—the authorities to choose team members, remove nonperformers, make assignments, and deliver some kind of performance consequences (especially the positive kind).

4 *Name the goal.*

Have a measurable goal and ruthlessly exclude irrelevant expenditures. Unlike congressional legislation, projects cannot become vehicles for irrelevant pork. The more clearly and measurably the project's goal is stated, the easier it will be for the project manager to stay focused and keep freeloaders off the bus.

5 *Plan the work and work the plan.*

A to-do list is not a plan and a schedule is not a plan, but both are a start. The length and depth of the plan will likely depend on the size and complexity of the project. Regardless of size, every plan should provide information that answers all the basic project questions: Why does the project exist? What will the project deliver? How will the project be done? Who will do the work? When will it be done? How much will it cost?

6 *Say how.*

The answer to "how" will likely require the most effort and ink. It's because this portion of the plan must spell out all necessary tasks (a breakdown of the work), their interdependencies, and deliverables. Don't forget to include tasks for the not-so-obvious work such as stakeholder management, communication to the organization, and risk mitigation.

7 *Check in frequently.*

The project manager usually needs to meet with project team members weekly to assess progress and make course corrections. Likewise, the executive who launched the project — and presumably has something to gain by its success — should meet with the project manager often for the same reasons.

8 *Make conscious trade-offs between good, fast, and cheap.*

Speaking of the executive who launched the project — usually called "sponsor" in project parlance — it is that person's job to make strategic trade-offs as the project proceeds. Projects almost never proceed exactly the way everybody hoped, so someone (the sponsor) has to consciously decide: "OK, we'll push the deadline out a month." Or, "Let's go ahead and increase the budget by 10 percent." Or, "Maybe we need to be a little less ambitious about what we're trying to achieve here." The point is that these trade-offs will be made. It's always better if the sponsor makes them consciously, rather than someone else making the trade-offs, or letting them happen by default.

Two pitfalls are worth noting:

- Project management is not just for the geeks. Often, the most expensive and attention-grabbing portion of internal projects is the information technology portion. But that part is almost never solely sufficient to deliver the organizational value intended by the project. Good project management cannot be confined to the information technology department, though it often is. It must extend to the project's success over the entire range of contributions, which may involve training, recruitment, process design, and just about any other business activity that affects the project's success. This means the project manager and her project must address all the affected parts of the business, not just the most expensive one.
- Don't confuse project management software with project management. Just as power saws don't turn woodmanglers into carpenters and spreadsheet software doesn't turn financial illiterates into accountants, project management software doesn't turn anyone into a project manager. It only helps those who already have the skills.

There is a brass ring for organizations that apply sound project management principles to all their projects. It is not just success on a given initiative; it's greater organizational agility, and ultimately greater ability to implement their own strategies.

THE POINT

Build the skills to manage projects across the organization and — maybe most of all — know when to use them.

4 ORGANIZATIONAL CULTURE AND CHANGE

Five Steps to Build a More Response-able Organization

People who correctly perceive the role they play in their own lives are generally able to respond well to life's challenges and opportunities. These *response-able* people tend to experience greater success and happiness than others who do not link their thoughts and behaviors to their outcomes. If you think that this distinction sounds like psychology, then you're right. Psychologist Julian Rotter developed a famous theory along these lines that divides people into two basic types.

The first is the external locus of control (ELOC) types, people who perceive the control over their lives as external to themselves ("I couldn't help it; she made me angry"). The second is the "internal locus of control" (ILOC) types, people who perceive control as internal to themselves ("Next time I'll count to ten before shooting off my mouth").

It's not hard to imagine that ILOCers fare better than ELOCers, as hundreds of studies have shown.

Likewise, teams and organizations comprised mostly of ILOCers succeed more often than those comprised mostly of ELOCers. Complaints about economic conditions, government regulations, or shareholders may all be valid, but complaining is rarely useful. One of our friends calls this kind of kvetching "admiring the problem."

Studies show the ILOC position offers greater resistance to stress, improved goal attainment, ability to learn from mistakes, and a de-emphasis on blame (including self-blame).

If you lead an organization, you should care about building a team of ILOCers. These five steps will take you there.

1 *Screen job candidates for their locus of control.*

Tests for LOC exist, but you don't really need them. (If you insist, you can obtain free ones online; just search on "locus of control test.") You can get a good notion of someone's LOC just by listening.

In the interview process, ask how they have handled relevant challenges and then take note of whether they whine and deflect blame, or instead discuss proactive solutions and lessons learned. Also notice how they talk about their previous employers. If someone thinks their three previous bosses were jerks, they are likely to think the same about you.

2 *Assign outcomes, not activities.*

When you assign someone a to-do list, you prescribe a solution — your solution, not theirs. But when you assign an outcome, you offer a problem — something for them to get their teeth into. Do you want list-followers or problem-solvers? Developing ILOC is, in part, about developing the habit of problem solving. If you do all the problem solving yourself, your subordinates will lose or fail to develop problem-solving skills.

Good leaders play the edge, experimenting with how large an assignment each individual can handle. The goal is to assign tasks that are big enough to challenge, but not big enough to overwhelm. Obviously, employees new to a task might need to discuss how to do something, but others should need to discuss only what must be accomplished and why.

3. *Manage what you have.*

   Unless you were lucky enough to pick your entire team, chances are you have inherited some ELOCers along with the ILOCers. Until you can reshape the makeup of your team, you will need to manage what you have.

   A key to managing ELOCers successfully is to understand how quickly they see obstacles and how oblivious they are to options. Often, when they discover an "obstacle" they will abandon the assignment altogether and may not even tell you. If they believe something can't be done, they will likely see no point in discussing it. To avoid this outcome, give them shorter assignments and check in more frequently. The previous guideline about assigning large tasks does not apply to hardcore ELOCers.

   For your ILOCers, the opposite is the recipe for success. They will appreciate the freedom to tackle their challenges, as long as they first understand the results you want.

4. *Reinforce ILOC behavior but not ELOC behavior.*

   Here's a life secret. When you allow employees to chronically produce excuses instead of results, you are encouraging unproductive ELOC behavior. By repeatedly making this one mistake you risk turning an effective organization into a stupid, whiney bureaucracy.

The antidote: Display scant interest in non-result-oriented, non-resourceful gobbledygook. You don't have to punish it, just don't feed it. Instead, give your nod to proactive problem solving and honest lessons well learned. At the very least, team members who fall in between the two approaches will start leaning toward the ILOC side.

5 *Model ILOC behavior yourself.*

It is not in speeches and memos that employees find out who you really are, but rather in your moments of exasperation or exhaustion. If your team sees you blame your boss, then they have permission to blame you. If they hear you whine about customers, expect them to start treating customers as intrusions — intrusions to their work. Instead, let them see you focus on what you need to do next, not on who ought to be lynched next.

You can learn to control what you say in those unguarded moments of frustration by better controlling what you say in your most important conversations, the ones you have with yourself. These are the conversations where you shape your character, including your locus of control.

Ultimately, building ILOC into your organization helps everybody. A response-able organization is saner, more productive, and more fun than any alternative. It's nice to know that, as a leader, there's plenty you can do to make that happen.

Create a Culture of Candor

NASA paid heavy tuition with the historic *Challenger* disaster. But it slept through class and paid tuition again with the *Columbia* debacle. The lesson: It's bad news when bad news can't make it to the top.

Cultures of denial do not work.

Little problems become big problems and big problems become catastrophes. These are the cultures in which executives either shoot the messengers of bad news or trivialize them as not being on board, not being team players, or simply not "getting it," whatever that means.

There are three causes for the culture of denial. The chief one is our natural human tendency to put off pain. Many of us would rather risk a root canal later than a drilled tooth now. That's why some executives condemn people who predict failure but tolerate those who fail.

In such cultures, executives will shun employees who realistically appraise a project as undoable with given resources. But employees who knowingly accede to unrealistic commitments — and then fail — are left alone or even hailed for their futile, eleventh-hour efforts.

Another contributor to the culture of denial is the confusion between bobble-headed yes-persons and genuine team contributors. Machiavelli wisely warned that successful leaders must surround themselves with people whose loyalty includes candid dissent. Richard Nixon's failure to do so arguably led to his downfall.

Whiners are a third factor: It is hard to not shoot the whining messenger. These bearers of bad news take smug delight in pointing out the iceberg ahead. Or, they spew negativity, figuring that endless venting is somehow good for the soul. But public executions of whiners will silence innocent employees who might otherwise have spoken up constructively.

How do you turn a culture of denial into a culture of candor? Here are seven ways.

1 *Teach employees to distinguish between bad news worth delivering and negative trivia worth forgetting.*

   What's important is to use multiple, realistic examples in both categories. People infer from examples far better than from bromides such as, "Use common sense." If you do offer a rule of thumb, here's a good one: When there's real impact to the organization, then it's definitely worth discussing.

2 *Teach employees to frame problems as business problems.*

   "Suzy and Debbie are really mad at each other," might best be teed up as, "I think we're headed for a productivity problem in collections."

3 *Teach employees that you want to hear bad news in a way that says, "We're in this together, and I want to help."*

   The distinction between the hand-wringing naysayer and the sharp-eyed lookout is often no more than one of approach. Most executives will warm to the messenger who aims at collaborating on a solution, not merely dumping a problem.

We had a dog once, Eddie, who killed a rat, brought it into the house, dropped it on our bed, and then stood there, howling and peeing, to prove his little doggy manhood. Bad dog.

But that might also describe the employee who prides herself on bringing you impressive problems — with no solutions. This isn't what you want. For such cases, it's well worth preaching another old rule: People who bring problems must also bring solutions.

Some successful leaders require employees to bring at least two solutions, on the belief that the first solution is usually an uncreative statement of the obvious.

4 *Timing counts.*

It's better to hear about time bombs before they explode. One savvy Fortune 50 CIO coaxes his people to tip him off to trouble with internal clients soon enough that he can help fix the problem, instead of too late to save the relationship. Such coaching is an ongoing chore, he says.

5 *Instruct employees about whom to inform, for what kind of issue.*

Because vital information often gets caught in the tar pit of middle management, state guidelines for when to go directly to senior management. For example, "If we are headed for a problem with a major customer — or a problem with lots of our smaller customers — come see me immediately, and bring some ideas about how to address the problem. Otherwise, work with your immediate supervisor."

6 *Use public praise and private correction to build the culture of candor.*

It's hard to think about praising skillful messengers of bad news when your attention has been commandeered by crisis. But it pays to briefly take focus off your calamity du jour and consciously thank the person who alerted you to it, especially if they entered with ideas for action, too. Better still is to mention that person's contribution in a meeting or memo, pointing out that they "helped us see the problem and create the solution."

When employees deliver bad news that is too late, too trivial, or without suggested solutions, explain what you would like from them next time. Focus on the future. Be clear. Use examples. Do it in private.

7 *Instead of shooting messengers, shoot people who shoot messengers.*

And whiners. You can shoot them too; just do it quietly.

Organizational Change – Getting Everybody on Board

Everybody wants things to be better but nobody wants them to be different. Getting people to want to do things differently is the problem executives face when they attempt any major improvement.

Most employees aren't thrilled with restructuring, downsizing, new systems, and constantly shifting strategies — all of which are daily fare these days. Executives often wonder, "What's the big deal with a little change?" But compared with other employees, executives have the advantage. They get a chance to roll the idea around in their heads for awhile, toss it back and forth among themselves, and come to grips with why it is necessary — and why other options won't do. After they've got the heft and feel of the new thing, it all seems obvious.

They're ready for action, now. So … why isn't everybody else?

Coaxing change from reluctant employees is never easy and it's often frustrating. But there are some guidelines that make the leaders' work a little less tough and a lot more successful. Here are nine that we've seen work well.

1 *Communicate until you're sick of it, and then communicate some more.*

Use different means to communicate the same message: e-mail, voice mail broadcasts, all hands meetings, conference calls, internal web sites, and so on.

The more complex or emotionally charged the message, the more redundancy you need. Complex or emotionally charged messages also mean that "lean" communication, such as e-mail and bulletin boards, cannot stand on their own. "Rich" communication such as one-on-ones and small brown bag sessions are necessary.

2 *Silence is deadly.*

If you've got nothing to say yet, then say that. "We thought we'd have the cuts figured out by now, but it's harder than we thought so we're taking another week to get it right."

If you don't want to eviscerate your middle management, tell them about the change before you tell everybody else. Give them the inside track. Worried about leaks? Tell the managers on Monday and tell everybody else on Tuesday. Then keep communicating.

3 *Measure improvement and share the results.*

There are two kinds of improvement to measure. Measure the change effort itself, such as whether the plan is on schedule, and then as soon as practical, the point of the improvement. If you're rolling out a quality program, for instance, don't just measure how many people have been trained. Also measure savings, error rate or something else that points to project success. All of these results are important pieces of information to share — with everybody.

4 *Involve employees in the effort.*

If you can't involve them in crafting the goal of the change (not usually necessary), then involve them in how the goal will be achieved. If you can't do that, then involve them in how your plans will be rolled out. If there are too many employees to actively involve them all, then create opportunities for them to volunteer their input. That might include something as simple as a voice mailbox for people to leave their ideas. Will there be cranks and naysayers? Sure, though the bigger threat to executive egos is the fact that employees' ideas will often trump their own (speaking from personal experience).

5 *Manage change like a project.*

Don't make the mistake of relegating change management to some junior clerk in Human Resources. Every element of a transition plan needs to be handled like a NASA launch, with time frames and accountabilities spelled out and managed by a competent project manager.

6 *Make the case for change.*

The rationale for change doesn't include only a compelling vision. Vision by itself won't dislodge most people from their comfort zones. Equally important is the compelling threat: What bad things will happen if we don't change?

Compelling threats don't work by telling employees that they're screwing up. Instead, compelling threats honor past practices while showing that such behavior will no longer work. In other words, "We're standing on a burning platform; this used to be a great place to stand, but now it's suicidal."

7 *Mobilize executive ranks before mobilizing the troops.*

It doesn't matter which honcho sponsors the change, even

if it's the top dog. If a critical mass of executives isn't on board, the change is going nowhere. How do you get them on board? Involve them in the early thinking. Get their fingerprints all over the plan. Executives who feel bypassed become huge obstacles down the road.

8 *Leverage your own accountability systems.*

If you have a system for goal-setting or performance management, align it with the new order. You don't want people getting bonuses for doing something the old way while you're pleading with them to do it the new way. A well-leveraged accountability system aligns the interests of the employees with the goals of the organization.

9 *Look through employees' eyes.*

Launch your change knowing that many good employees will hold beliefs you might dismiss. You say, "Improve the process," but they may think, "Trim the payroll." You say, "Improve our hiring practices," and they may think, "So. We're not good enough?"

Fortunately, most people will follow a leader who leads with their perspective in mind. To do that, you will need to demonstrate an understanding of perspectives that you may not approve of, and do that without disapproving of the people who hold those perspectives.

It's easy for leaders burdened with the complexity and costs of an organizational change to neglect the change process itself. But these nine guidelines are really just leadership on steroids. They're all good leadership habits anytime, and particularly in times of change.

Transformational Levers for Big Organizational Change

Theories on change management abound. This isn't one of them. It's a simple checklist for anyone driving big, complex organizational change. But first, you have to recognize when you are facing what we'll call "Big Change."

Some examples: You are swapping out leaders, and the new boss is bringing new "direction." You are downsizing or consolidating. You are fixing an organization-wide problem with maintenance, safety, or something equally broad. Or, you are moving the location of a factory. The list is endless, but you get the picture.

There are two sides to the Big Change coin (pun intended). There is the "hard side," the physical details that will — or had better — end up in a project plan, complete with pretty Gantt charts. The other side of the coin is the "soft side," the people stuff. Of course, it's the soft side of change management that makes Big Change hard. And if you think that the soft side is too squishy to be managed in any hardheaded way, you might be surprised. (And for Pete's sake, don't try to get off the hook by appointing a "change manager." If you're leading the change, *you* are the change manager!)

There is a handful of "people systems" that can be your transformational levers on the soft side of Big Change. If these people systems are aimed in the same direction as your change, you'll probably succeed. But if they are pointed in a different direction, then it's like driving a car with its wheels out of alignment — while you're steering in one direction, invisible forces pull you in a different direction.

This checklist enumerates eight ways to harness those invisible forces and makes them available as transformational levers. The point is to put transformational levers in your plan alongside "select moving company." You want to get all the arrows to point in the same direction at the right time.

Most of these levers can be used to get you through the change, and they can also be used on the other side of the change to sustain it. Here, we are talking about just using them to get you through the change itself. For example, the first lever, Measurement, could remind you to measure how many people are trained in a new process, how many have adopted the new process, how much rework is required as they get used to the new process, and so on.

We call this our MICE ROAR checklist (thanks to Jeff Kenyon, software guru and graduate of our Implementing Strategic Change course, for sorting our list into a clever acronym). As you read the list, think about how you might use it to get through a big change.

Measurement

Involvement

Communication

Education & Training

Reinforcement

Organizational Structure

Accountability Processes

Resourcing

- *Measurement.*

  "What gets measured gets done" isn't exactly true — it's performance consequences that best influence performance. However, there is no better spotlight or foundation for consequences than measurement. You can measure processes (how well you are doing what you say you're doing) or you can measure outcomes (the results of your processes).

- *Involvement.*

  Most change management researchers agree that involvement of people affected by the change is important. The underlying reason: People hate feeling out of control during important phases of their lives. In a change project, this discomfort quickly leads to resistance. To avoid this, give people affected by the change a serious opportunity to influence the nature of the change and how it is implemented, and you must take their ideas seriously. At the same time, "Opportunity" does not mean that everybody must share their opinions, "Influence" does not mean control, and "Ideas taken seriously" does not mean always getting one's way.

- *Communication.*

  Generalized resistance to change occurs when people feel out of control, and it is magnified by anxiety generated by not knowing what's going on. The problem is that people don't hear well when they're resisting, and their uncertainty doesn't go away when rational explanations are offered. If anything, resistance increases, causing further escalation of anxiety and resistance. The only way to break this vicious circle is communication, and lots of it! (As a good starting point, consider William Bridges's 7x7 principle: Communicate it seven times, seven different ways. His wise book, *Managing Transitions*, is highly recommended.)

- *Education.*

  People must be educated about the transformational change and trained on the skills to execute it. Education and training is straightforward. It simply means that people must be knowledgeable about the vision, values, goals, and objectives of the organization, and must be equipped with the skills necessary for their new jobs. Keep in mind the principle of just-in-time training: Don't teach people how to do something waaayyyy before they'll be able to use it. They just forget.

- *Reinforcement.*

  We all know that people tend to do what they are rewarded for doing. It's pretty obvious that the reinforcement system needs to be changed whenever there's a strategic change to the work that people do. We take a broad view of the reinforcement system, and include in it the way people get paid (and what they get paid for), their benefits, other financial rewards, and nonfinancial forms of reward and recognition.

- *Organizational structure.*

  This refers to three things:

1. *Accountability hierarchy* (the lines and boxes on an organizational chart, who's accountable to whom for what)
2. *Process design* (the lines and boxes on a process flow chart)
3. *Position descriptions* (If you have names that you plan to match with positions, include them). As with all transformational tools, you will have some elements that you install only during the change and some that will endure after it. Therefore, you will have some organizational structure considerations that are temporary — say, the design of the project team. And you will have some design considerations that are permanent, such as the design of the organization being changed.

- *Accountability processes.*

  These are the processes by which you hold people accountable — they are sometimes referred to as performance management. Implementation of strategic change, by definition, affects the work for which people are held accountable. During periods of change, it is especially crucial to have processes to ensure the three elements of accountability (Clear Request, Commitment, and Consequences for Performance, as we described earlier in "The Three C's of Accountability.")

  During the change you will need more frequent goal setting and shorter goal review intervals. During a big change with the entrenched staff of a not-for-profit organization, we found weekly review intervals to be especially helpful in turning things around. As the change took root, monthly intervals sufficed. (For more on this topic, see the earlier chapter, "How to Make Strategy Review = Strategy Execution.")

- *Resourcing.*

  Resourcing is about getting the right people into the right jobs, either by external recruitment or through internal postings. It also includes succession planning. Big change often shifts the requirements of key positions, calling for different personal attributes and skills by the people in those positions. When it does, resourcing efforts need to have been thought out in advance and kicked into gear. For this reason, even a downsizing might require some additional hiring.

USING THE MICE ROAR CHECKLIST

We hope you found the MICE ROAR checklist a useful way to organize your thinking around the soft side of big change. But the list isn't intended simply as "good stuff to keep in mind."

So, here's our parting suggestion. When you are in the planning phase of a big change, gather your planning team together to focus on these transformational levers. Take each lever, one at a time, and brainstorm the actions required to align your people systems with the change you intend. This is the kind of due diligence and planning that makes transformational change actually deliver on its promise.

5 INNOVATION

When Failure Leads to Innovation, and When It Doesn't

Success requires experimentation and successful experimentation requires an eagerness to learn from failure. The entrepreneur's challenge can be summed up as ensuring that the *learn rate* exceeds the *burn rate*. Those who don't learn fast enough go under.

INSTRUCTIVE FAILURE VERSUS TERMINAL FAILURE

Early on, Hewlett Packard exploited the power of instructive failure. According to Peter Sims, "Hewlett Packard cofounder Bill Hewlett said HP needed to make 100 small bets on products to identify six that could be breakthroughs. So, little bets are for learning about problems and opportunities while big bets are for capitalizing on them once they've been identified." These "small bets" are what we would call experiments: exposure to nonfatal failure that teaches you something.

On the other hand, Circuit City was an electronics store chain that failed terminally because it hadn't had enough instructive failures. After leading the industry in the 1980s and 1990s, the company became complacent and stopped experimenting. It missed the boat on the gaming market, didn't take advantage of in-store promotions from companies like Apple, and failed to improve its Internet sales, leaving room for the more innovative rival Best Buy to take the lead. By the time Circuit City tried to pull out of its nosedive, the failure had become terminal.

Deliberate, inquisitive exposure to failure is an experiment. And a clever experiment is like a clever investment — your downside (risk) is manageable and your upside (lesson) is spectacular. Of course, there is a time to bet the farm, but that's only after you've learned which farm to bet.

DUMB FAILURE

What's the difference between failure that's experimentation and failure that is merely failure? Maybe this: If you make a nonfatal mistake and learn from it, then it is "experimentation." But if you make a mistake and then deflect its lessons, then it is simply a failure. Lessons learned lead to innovation; lessons flunked, as in school, tend to be repeated.

Here are some ways to flunk at failing:

- *Finger pointing.*

  When the question is, "Who screwed up?" instead of "What did we learn?" then the only thing that's learned is how to keep your head down.

- *Reasons, stories, and excuses.*

  When an organization's lousy results allegedly stem from "the poor economy," or "difficulty finding talent," or "tough competition," then nothing is learned or even speculated about what the organization can do better. Part of Warren Buffet's initial fame stemmed from the annual reports in which he gave blunt assessments of what he and Berkshire Hathaway could have done better. It showed shareholders that lessons were not squandered.

- *Unclear success.*

  Like a scientist with an untestable hypothesis, a leader

with an unclear goal can spend a lot of time and money without learning much. For example, when any given organization consolidates two departments in order to "capture synergies," what does "synergies" mean? Lower costs? Faster product development? Quicker response? *What*? Without a clear goal, you don't even know when you've failed.

- *Activity-based success.*

  Of course, you can be clear about your success, but rather than defining it as a result, you define it as an activity or expenditure of money or other resources. In that case, failure and learning are equally unlikely. This is because no hypothesis is tested. For example, government officials often declare success after they have launched programs or increased spending. Costs go up, but learning stays flat.

All these problems function as organizational learning disabilities, dysfunctions that block learning. And when learning is blocked, so is innovation.

SMART FAILURE

Failure is inevitable, but you can choose whether it is instructive or terminal. Henry Ford said that failure is the opportunity to begin again, more intelligently. But many of us begin again with no increase in intelligence. Or we don't get smarter because we won't risk failure in the first place.

On their quest for "smart failure," innovators must focus on two dimensions. First, increase the rate of nonfatal failure with small, fast steps. In his pre-political days, New York Mayor Michael

Bloomberg founded Bloomberg L.P., a vast business media empire. When asked how his corporation managed to complete such large information technology projects, he replied that they were successful precisely because they did not undertake large projects; they undertook lots of little projects. It's better to get your grand plans 60 percent right and then start an execution cycle of rapid, small steps that makes you smarter, faster — adjust and refine the plan along the way. Design firm IDEO expresses this approach in their company slogan, "Fail often in order to succeed earlier."

Second, increase the amount learned from failure. When an employee takes an educated whack at a problem and the problem remains unsolved, that employee and her boss are at a crossroads. One path is to deflect responsibility — it was someone else's fault. The other, better path is to pick the bone clean, with the employee learning every possible lesson from the "tuition" paid. Better yet, the lesson gets spread and learning is celebrated so that everyone in the team, department, or organization goes to school on one person's tuition. One nuclear engineer, a submariner, told us, "We celebrate little problems because that's where we learn how to avoid the big ones."

ADVICE FOR INNOVATIVE LEADERS

Leaders can improve their organizations' performance on both dimensions — frequency of productive failure and amount learned per failure — with some reasonably simple straightforward techniques.

- *Make learning — rather than performing — the first task.*

  Good management consultants always enter the uncharted waters of a project with a "discovery phase" before the "performance phase." Goal researchers have found that performance improves on difficult tasks if your initial aim is simply to learn how to perform the task. You have to learn what you need to do before you try to do it.

- *Nix projects that do not sharply define their intended outcomes.*

  Without a crystal-clear target, too much after-the-fact rationalization creeps in — and then everything is an alleged success, and nobody learns anything. Although the path to your destination may be unclear, the destination shouldn't be. So, for example, the next time someone wants to reorganize a department, ask him exactly what outcomes he'd like to produce, what side effects he'd like to avoid, and how he'll know if he's been successful. Press hard for precision and measurable results.

  If, along your path to clear results, you decide on a different destination, that's fine. Just be clear about that destination, too.

- *Watch your language.*

  Call innovation projects "experiments" or "learning pilots." Make it clear from the onset that the point is to figure out what works, or at very least figure out what doesn't work. You can't just give people "permission to fail and learn." That permission has to permeate your language.

- *Limit your losses.*

  Target initial efforts that won't kill you if they fail. For example, if you have a theory that putting a design team and an engineering team under one boss will produce more marketable products, then try one project that does just that. Don't change the whole organization until you've lowered your risks by upping your knowledge. Think "fast, small, and low risk."

- *Banish happy talk.*

  Demonstrate that you are looking for truth, not Prozac. And don't punish the truth-tellers. When Alan Mulally took over as Ford's president and CEO in 2006, he was quickly fed up with deflected lessons that dodged both learning and accountability. As *The Economist* tells the story: "He asked managers to color-code their progress reports — ranging from green for good to red for troubled. At one early meeting he expressed astonishment at being confronted by a sea of green, even though the company had lost several billion dollars in the previous year. Ford's recovery began only when he got his managers to admit that things weren't entirely green."

- *Embrace disproof before you embrace proof.*

  Rather than task your team to prove that an idea works, task them to disprove it instead. For example, if a vendor you love has a new "solution," find where it fails instead of looking for evidence that it works. Scientific philosopher Karl Popper taught the world that people get smarter by trying to disconfirm our theories rather than by looking for cases where we are right. The point of experimentation is to get smarter, not to be right.

- *Make "Aha!" and "Doh!" part of every progress brief.*

  While you look to your subordinates for results, also look to them for learning. When people brief the boss (that's you), they need to know that part of the achievement for an "A" is to share discoveries. If all you get is happy talk, then prodding is in order. "Surely not everything has gone well. What have you learned from the glitches?" Assume glitches and applaud learning.

- *Turn "lessons learned" into "lessons applied."*

  Require that plans for new initiatives demonstrate how they incorporate learning from past initiatives. One of us (Wendi) did that with project managers whose "lessons learned" exercise had become a useless bureaucratic gesture. When "lessons learned" become "lessons applied," it leads to consistently smarter, more innovative projects.

Rapid, ongoing innovation demands that leaders treat intellectual capital like any other capital. Accumulate it, nurture it, and use it. Requisite to this game is the organizational capability for frequent, productive failure. And that kind of smart failure requires smart leadership.

We Can All Play in the "Innovation Sandbox"

"Innovation sandbox" is a term coined by the late C.K. Prahalad. It's gist is this: For a truly quantum innovation in either goods or services, (1) set a really high bar for what "good" looks like, (2) identify a small handful of aggressive constraints, and then, within that "sandbox" (3) begin a radical reexamination of your assumptions and self-imposed limits as you develop your breakthrough design. That combination forces you, as Apple says, to "think different."

Prahalad's many examples focus on impoverished markets at the "base of the pyramid" (BOP), where the average person earns a couple of bucks a day. He describes innovations in cars, hotels, communications, and other areas that achieve world-class quality, yet remain affordable to society's poorest — and turn a great profit for the entrepreneurs providing them. Now, that's sustainability!

One example Prahalad describes is absolutely world-class cardiac surgery costing $1500 (including profit) that is the equivalent of $45,000 surgery in the United States. Oh, and he describes a companion product, innovative health insurance, also profitable, that enables entire villages in India to have access to the surgery and other medical services, when needed.

A high bar, aggressive constraints, and radical reexamination all spur dramatic innovation, again and again.

But the innovation sandbox that Prahalad describes isn't just for wealthy entrepreneurs and multinationals serving vast third world markets. Actually, anyone can play in the sandbox. We were reminded of this recently in a conversation with our friend, Pamela Giusto-Sorrells, the president of Pamela's Products, a producer of popular gluten-free foods.

Pam loves developing products, and she loves a good challenge. One product she is feeling good about is her single-serve, gluten-free brownie mix for kids. Watch for the sandbox in this plucky lady's own words:

> "A lot of other bakers think that gluten-free products have to taste like sawdust, and I literally grew up in a health food industry that believed that. But it's just plain wrong. I've spent a lot of time developing gluten-free recipes that taste really great.
>
> So here was my latest challenge: You raise your children on a gluten-free diet, and then you send them off to college and their buddies are doing something else, eating pizza, pretzels, cookies, and whatever else other teenagers eat. Unfortunately, a lot of their snacks will make the gluten-intolerant kid sick.
>
> So my goal was to make something gluten-free that the wheat-eating college kid wants to eat. It's got to be that good. So, first I asked myself, what does everybody like? Chocolate. What's a great all-American food? Brownies. People love brownies. They're a perfect late-night snack. But I had to work within constraints.
>
> For cooking, college kids probably have only a microwave; but I figured that they can get water from the bathroom, and they can keep a bottle of oil in their dorm rooms. It's all about making really great food with limited resources.

> So, how do I do it with limited resources? Take our brownie mix, package 100 grams, and mix in two tablespoons of oil and two tablespoons of water. Everybody's got a spoon. Everybody's got a bowl or a mug to mix it in. And everybody's got 60 seconds — one minute to instant gratification. Because it's so fast and easy, kids show it to other kids and — *et voilà*! — the wheat-eaters are eating the gluten-free kid's snacks. Touchdown!"

Clever Soviet engineer Genrich Altshuller asserted that invention arises from apparent contradiction. Say you want an object to be heavy duty but also lightweight, or cheap but also sturdy, and so on. Invention, Altshuller explained, is always a resolution of apparent contradictions such as these. But C.K. Prahalad went further and at a more universal level: It is the apparent contradiction between a lofty goal and severe constraints that energizes our most innovative thinking, as long as we are willing to scrutinize — and change — our assumptions about what's possible.

Lessons Learned About Lessons Learned

Even good organizations can seem incredibly dumb. This is especially obvious when they make the same mistakes again and again, or don't exploit what they know. As with people, even the smartest among us can have occasional learning disabilities.

Learning disabilities are costly in organizations. Consider the telco that made a multimillion-dollar mistake when one division picked an inept supplier for a project and then another division hired the same nincompoops a few months later for a different project.

Then there was the construction company that couldn't get its biggest customer to pay on time. And even though one of the company's regional offices finally cracked the code on getting timely payment, none of the other offices got the message.

The standard antidote to these organizational learning disabilities is the "lessons learned" meeting, in which employees share what's working and what's not. But although these meetings are a good idea in concept, their track record is spotty.

Those two companies held lessons-learned meetings, but to no effect. Often the assemblies turned into gripe sessions or yielded information that was later ignored or inaccessible.

But if your organization is willing to treat lessons learned as a matter of strategic importance, a lessons-learned process can become a useful tool. Here are five lessons we've learned about effective "lessons learned."

1. *Set a policy for when to trigger lessons-learned meetings.*

   The policy will need to apply to both projects and day-to-day operations.

   Most projects should be launched with a review of previous lessons learned and should end with lessons learned meetings of their own. Large projects also should use major milestones as trigger points. It's not smart to wait until the project's end for the lessons learned meeting. Too much will have been forgotten and too many opportunities missed.

   For day-to-day work, you are not likely to have event-driven triggers, so you need to establish a calendar-driven process. Set regular, cross-functional lessons-learned meetings, or fold the topic into an existing, recurring meeting. An organization's own employees are often its best consultants, but only if they are encouraged to talk with each other.

2. *Design your lessons-learned process to dig deep for employee contributions.*

   For example, some projects have so many participants that you will get more ideas with a survey than a large, unwieldy meeting.

   When meetings do make the most sense, they will benefit from structured, facilitated brainstorming. Be sure the process is designed to capture both avoidable mistakes and exploitable successes for next time.

Another way to increase the amount of usable information is to gather it into standardized categories and a standardized format. Participants will contribute far more when asked to think of lessons learned about one targeted topic at a time, such as client, technology, pricing process, and so on. In addition, users of the lessons learned structure will find the data much easier to review when the format doesn't change from project to project.

Keeping a positive tone will help you mine even more useful content. While you certainly want to capture "Mistakes to Avoid," you also need to capture "Successes Worth Repeating." And even when discussing and documenting problem areas, keep in mind that the point is to influence future action. Stay focused on next time and on the things that can actually be affected by the people in your organization.

3 *Create a lessons-learned knowledge bank.*

Employees should know there is one place within their organization where all lessons learned reside. Whether this is at the corporate level or lower depends on how widely applicable the lessons are.

Then be sure to assign an employee as keeper of this corporate asset. This person's job is to ensure the accessibility and integrity of the data. (In project-based organizations, this work probably belongs in the project management office.)

4 *Make employees accountable for using your lessons learned process.*

If you believe that embedding organizational learning is important, then hold people accountable for making it happen. Imbed this accountability at the individual level and on two fronts.

First, there must be accountability for feeding the lessons-learned repository, creating data for future use. A leader who is not making contributions is either learning nothing or contributing nothing of what she learns.

Second, imbed accountability for actually using those past lessons. You want plenty of withdrawals from your lessons-learned bank, not just deposits.

Make these accountabilities explicit — reflected in performance appraisals, project launch templates, quality checklists, and so on.

5 *Communicate your successes.*

As the repository of lessons learned increases — and as people use it — successes will unavoidably result. Record those successes, then communicate them throughout the organization.

You will be celebrating the heroes who profitably participated in the system. You will also ensure continued company-wide support for stamping out organizational learning disability.

6 ORGANIZATIONAL STRUCTURE

Restructuring Requires Smart Tactics

Leaders in the U.S. administration say the economy is getting better, and we'd love to believe it. But we still see plenty of belt-tightening out there, some of it smart and some of it not-so-smart.

Both smart and not-so-smart cost cutting frequently takes the form of organizational redesign. Although employees roll their eyes at these initiatives, they really are often the best way to accomplish more with less.

Here's the problem. When most executives consider restructuring, they tend to think at a level that is lofty, strategic, and high-level. But they often give no more than a nod to the nitty-gritty decisions about who will be accountable to whom and what the work will look like. Those decisions are no less important than decisions to centralize or decentralize, or to insource or outsource. If the tactics don't work, the strategy doesn't matter.

The tactics of good organizational design are simple to understand, if not easy to execute. Here are four that spell the difference between successful and unsuccessful structural change.

1 *Get the work processes right before you start drawing organizational charts.*

   If your organization is of any size, you have work processes such as order fulfillment or product development that have evolved over time, like that mess in your garage or your top desk drawer. If you want to cut costs, first figure out how the work flows today ("This happens, then that happens …"), then figure out ways to eliminate, shorten, or combine steps. If you can't find significant savings, you're not trying hard enough.

Once you've designed smarter workflows, then you can start thinking about structure — who reports to whom. Remember, structure serves process, not the other way around. If all this is Greek to you, browse a copy of Rummler and Brache's *Improving Productivity*, a readable classic.

2 *Avoid absolute manager/subordinate ratios.*

Spreadsheet jockeys love the simplistic notion that there is an exact "right" span of control — the number of direct reports that a manager can handle. There isn't. To determine a position's span of control, ask yourself two questions. First, how much oversight will supervisees' roles demand? Chicken pluckers require less ongoing direction than system architects — one manager can probably handle more of the former than the latter. Second, how much time must the manager devote to nonsupervisory matters? If the sales manager is supposed to sell and manage, then she can handle fewer salespeople than when she is only managing.

3 *Make it flat, but not too flat.*

Tom Peters' ideal of an "infinitely flat organization" is infinitely silly. For organizations of any size, there will always be layers. That is a good thing. In a well-structured organization, the managers at one layer receive meaningful context from the managers above them, and in turn they provide it to the folks in the next layer down.

If you've ever had a boss who could not give you a bigger picture for your work than you could give yourself, then you know the frustrations and frictions that result. If that symptom is widespread, then your organization probably is ripe for flattening.

Excessively flat organizations are less common creatures, but they do exist. For example, that's when you're thinking, "How do I expand our distribution in the Pacific Northwest?" but your subordinate is hoping for help with her to-do list. Here, you're probably missing a layer or two.

Six decades of research support the notion that there is an exactly right number of layers for any given organization, but figuring out what that number is requires a little know-how. As we said earlier, if you want to know more, search online for "Elliott Jaques," the man who led this research.*

4 *Create no neutered management roles.*

Okay, here's the rule: If a role is accountable for the output of other employees, then it's a managerial role. Managerial roles must have managerial authorities, such as writing appraisals, approving raises, and so on. Otherwise, you cannot hold them accountable for what other employees do or how they do it.

* Write us at info@elg.net and we'll send you a few articles on Jaques and his research.

> That's pretty logical. But many new organizational designs sport a whole crop of "leadership" roles without authority. "Quality Champion," "Process Owner," and "Six Sigma Lead" are typical titles. People in these positions can educate, facilitate, or advocate. But they cannot manage. Therefore, don't expect people in these roles to produce results through other employees. (This is a career-clobbering problem, and we say more about it in the next chapter.)

All four of these principles — processes before structure, appropriate manager/subordinate ratios, right layering, and authorized managers — are the tactical matters that make good organizational design work. Without using them, it will be hard to know whether your brilliant new structure is as brilliant as you hope.

Accountability Without Authority: How to Drive Employees Crazy

Both hands flat on her desk, fingers splayed, Suzi looked up and glared before smiling weakly, in recognition. The last time we had seen her, two years previously, she looked ten years younger. Now, these thin lips and narrowed eyes belonged to a different person. She had lost her laugh — and much more. Suzi and others we have seen before and since, had been dragged through the No Authority Gauntlet — what we call the "NAG syndrome."

Here's how it's done: You hand someone a management job, but one without commensurate management authorities. In other words, make this person accountable for the work of others — but with no accompanying clout — and make sure that this pseudo-manager's accountability goes on for months or even years. The people "reporting" to the pseudo-manager must also have other managers with other demands, but those other managers must have actual, ordinary managerial authorities (selection, deselection, performance appraisal, and all the rest).

These employees may sincerely make commitments to this pseudo-manager and they may intend to keep those commitments as well. After all, it will be for a good cause — "quality," "customer service," "process improvement," "safety," or some such thing. The lip service will thus come easily and enthusiastically. However, when it's time to prioritize work, these employees will naturally prioritize the demands of their real managers ahead of those of the pseudo-manager. Thus begins the NAG syndrome.

THE THREE STAGES OF THE NAG SYNDROME

The pseudo-manager's NAG syndrome in three stages:

1 *Jubilance.*

In this initial state, the pseudo-manager is proud to be tackling a task that darn near everyone agrees is terribly important. She is confident that any organizational challenge can be met. Huzzah!

2 *Doubt.*

Lip service and elbow grease seem to be going in different directions. People keep endorsing the pseudo-manager's task, but follow-through is sporadic. The pseudo-manager can't understand what's going on and neither can anyone else. Not enough leadership? Not enough communication?

3 *Bitterness.*

This is the final, crazy, phase. In the face of flaccid cooperation — or even rebellion — the pseudo-manager becomes indignant. Don't these people understand how important this is? Don't they care about the organization? Weren't promises made?

Cleaving to the importance of her task, like a believer in a land of apostates, the pseudo-manager uses the only authority she has: NAG authority. She becomes a total pain in the rear — if she continues to take her mission seriously. That's the unfairness of it. Only pseudo-managers who take their tasks seriously are most affected by the NAG syndrome. Less dedicated souls find a way to bail out.

SLOWER, RISKIER, COSTLIER

In some organizations, NAG is practically synonymous with project management. A few years ago we conducted research on more than five hundred project managers and found that a huge contributor to project failure was the NAG syndrome, second only to unclear project goals. The problem is so endemic that courses are offered to project managers on how to manage without authority. That strikes us as similar to teaching people how to live with malaria instead of giving them mosquito nets. "Process management," likewise, has its share of failures because the "process owner" had no authority. Once the frothy-mouthed organizational enthusiasm dies down and the suit-clad consultants go away, nagging process owners find they cannot enforce the new quality process (or whatever) that cuts across the organization.

Organizations waste millions of dollars this way. Our research has shown that — best case — initiatives undertaken by nagging, pseudo-managers take waaaaaaay longer than initiatives undertaken by managers who have ordinary managerial authority.

Consider: We're talking about one of the really big risks to success, and yet it costs absolutely nothing to mitigate.

HOW IT ALL STARTS

It isn't a bad guy who usually launches a NAG scenario. Normally, these messes seem logical at the time. For example, you put one bright, articulate person in charge of monitoring some particular process — say, power consumption at various military installations. After awhile, she becomes the expert on power consumption at these facilities. At that point, then you say, "Hey, you're the expert on this. How about if you take the lead on decreasing power across all these facilities?" But she's not in command of any of these installations. She has no authority over anyone in any of them. Still: "Sure," she says, "I'll be happy to take the lead." And so she begins her march down the nagging path to nuttiness.

Too often we put faith in the cure called "communication" or the cure called "leadership." Because we know that these qualities are necessary, we believe them to be sufficient. They are sufficient only some of the time. The problem is the failure to distinguish what it takes to obtain occasional cooperation from others within the organization versus the conditions needed to do it all the time. This is the difference between borrowing a cup of sugar from a neighbor and shopping in his pantry. It's the difference between using your relationships and using them up.

Finally, we see NAG setups occurring when "everybody agrees" that "we've got to do something" about X. For example, at one telecommunication company, we happened to be talking with the "VP of Quality" right at the moment he was packing boxes in his office, preparing to move out. The company and all of its leadership had recognized the need to quickly and dramatically improve quality on a number of fronts. So they had hired a famous quality guru.

They had given him leeway to hire a handful of bright young internal consultants, which he had. They had given him an office next to the CEO. They had given him a substantial training budget to help get everyone trained on "quality." But after everyone had been trained, and after all the confetti and hoopla had settled down, quality essentially had gone nowhere.

Standing there in his office, we asked him: "Did you ever have the authorities you needed to do what you came to do — to actually get your peers to change how they operate?"

This bright and charismatic leader glowered a bit at the cheeky question. Then, taking a deep breath, he said, "No," and closed his eyes briefly.

The whole company had been in a frenzy over quality. Who would think the VP of Quality would need any clout? Why bother giving him the same sort of authorities that you would give the head of production, sales, shipping, or anything else? Heck, everyone is so enthusiastic about the cause, why bother with such nits at all?

Because they're required, that's all. (Or "requisite," as management guru Elliott Jaques would have said.)

All these goof-ups occur because they sometimes work. Like a failed gambling strategy, success comes now and then, despite lousy reasoning. Occasional success is just enough encouragement for executives to scrutinize a NAG-stricken pseudo-manager and conclude, "We've got to get someone in here who can lead!" Or, "We all just need to communicate better!"

CURING THE NAG

The solution to the problem of nonempowered managers is really quite simple. Downsize their accountability to match their miniscule authority, or upsize their authorities — publicly anointing them (people cannot self-anoint) — to match their accountability. Anything else should leave nagging doubts.

Matrix Management – and Three Rules that Make It Actually Work

Sometimes it helps to ask the right question. Several years ago, a client asked us for our advice on "matrix management," a technique of organizational structuring that at the time was new for many organizations. Here was our response:

Avoid it! It's a train wreck! In a matrix, the org chart goes in two or more directions — a matrix — and nobody knows who their boss is or which subordinate they can count on. Any organization claiming to do "matrix" is having big problems, no matter what they claim to the press.

This harsh criticism was based on responses we received when we asked people if they were "doing matrix" and, if so, how it was working. When their organizations were trying to use the matrix structure, they would also admit that it was a complete dog's breakfast.

However, the same client insisted on proceeding with a matrix approach. So we had to figure out whether anyone had succeeded with this approach and, if so, how.

It turned out that we had been asking the wrong question. The first thing we learned was to quit asking people about "matrix" (a fad term at the time) and instead ask them, "Do you have any employees with two or more bosses, and does that arrangement work?"

Many people said, "Sure, we do that." And then they would tell us how, which was how we learned what did and did not work. One surprising conclusion: we learned that when it works, the benefits are terrific.

One such benefit is that managers can share resources with other managers when their work requires representation from different parts of the business or it requires different kinds of expertise. Large, change-the-organization initiatives, such as core process re-engineering or a deep dive on solving a big problem, usually require different kinds of expertise, from different functions, under the same leader.

Also, there's a big cost advantage to being able to share expertise across departmental lines. If three departments can effectively share the same engineer, everybody wins, including the bottom line.

But pity the poor engineer and those three managers if the structure for sharing isn't set up right. That's the "train wreck," and it includes problems such as:

- *Employees receive conflicting directions.*

  Having multiple managers for the same employee often results in multiple directions for the same task. This situation leaves the employee in a no-win situation and is sure to upset at least one of the bosses.

- *With contradictory directions comes unclear leadership.*

  Who is in charge of what? Wherever the organization is trying to go, employees will be at a loss to follow.

- *Employees have unrealistic demands put on their time.*

When three managers each want 75 percent of one employee's time, something's got to give. Usually, the employee is forced to make de facto prioritization decisions for the three bosses, and those decisions are not always right for the organization.

- *Managers can't get their work done.*

  Often, the poor schlep with "dotted line" employees faces this mess. Every time he or she assigns work to an (in)direct report, that work competes with work from the "real" boss. Of course, the real boss is the one who actually does the employee's appraisals or exerts the most influence on the employee's next promotion.

Fortunately, these problems are not inevitable. In fact, we have interviewed managers in organizations who have shared resources for years with nary a glitch. These successful organizations are often professional service firms, including law, engineering, and architectural firms, as well as management consultants. The IT shop often gets it right and we even found one large hotel-restaurant company that cracked the code.

All of these organizations followed a set of simple, inflexible rules that can be applied by any organization to make resource-sharing productive and reasonably trouble-free. While some organizations used an internal customer-supplier approach, many of them used a system distinctly reminiscent of the way students are resource-shared across multiple teachers. In this common practice, students produce reports for one teacher, take a test for another, and run laps for a third.

Success rests on these three rules:

1. *No two managers can assign the same task to the same employee.*

   For example, an English teacher would not tell a student how to solve an equation, nor would an algebra teacher tell a student how to parse a sentence.

   If you have ever seen a coach and a parent shouting instructions to the same student athlete at the same time, you have seen this violation in action. If you have seen a project with two project managers, you have probably witnessed the same violation.

2. *Each manager must control meaningful performance consequences.*

   This is much like how each teacher must hand out grades for his or her own class. Imagine your kid's study habits if only one teacher handed out grades.

   Managers with dotted-line employees might wish that they, too, could hand out grades for the work they request. In successful organizations, they can — and it's treated as more than "input."

3. *Work overloads must be resolved by managers, not employees.*

   When three managers have each assigned a 75-percent workload to the same person, they — and not the employee — must resolve the conflict.

   An employee's only obligation is to notify the managers of the problem. How do you get employees to do that?

> "We hire grownups," wisecracked one wag at a law firm that handles the shared-resource problem particularly well. "The resource being allocated," he added, "is not in charge of resource allocation."
>
> It may also help that these non-partner grownups are firmly corrected if they unilaterally decide which partner's work gets done and which gets deferred. Some organizations even set up formal processes to identify and resolve such conflicts.

Maybe the most important fact we learned in our research is that the must-haves of successful matrix management are not really new. It has always been the case that employees function best when they know to whom and for what they are accountable, when they understand their priorities, and when they are rewarded for good performance. As it turns out, the rise of matrix management has not changed the fundamentals.

ADDENDUM

Here's a common twist associated with matrix management. Specialized knowledge workers such as database analysts are accountable to one manager for *how* they perform their work and to other managers for *what* work they perform. The "how" director, whom we call the "expertise manager," is empowered to preserve and improve each expert's expertise. This is a beautiful system that is all about multiplying the power of experts. "Multiplying the Power of Experts" is a free white paper on this topic.*

* You can find this white paper at: www.elg.net/articles

On Head Chopping

For years, we've preached the need to look deeper than simple head-count reduction when cutting costs. Of course, we don't deny that head count as a single-minded focus has its appeal.

For one thing, layoffs send a dramatic, belt-tightening message to the board and the public. Employee-to-revenue ratios inevitably improve, at least temporarily, which makes the stock analysts happy. And enforced layoffs provide reticent managers an excuse to finally clear out the deadwood.

Unfortunately, head-count reduction may also bear the appeal of protecting executive positions.

When you're counting jobs instead of labor costs, you're likelier to cut five productive but powerless peons than one useless but politically connected executive.

But our beef isn't with layoffs, it's with the boneheaded way executives decide on the numbers and positions to be jettisoned. The usual loose analysis yields the usual predictable disasters. Here are a few:

- *Reverse Darwinism.*

  When layoffs drag on too long, it's the least fit who stick around. The more talented employees seek saner employment elsewhere, while those with anemic résumés wait behind, fearfully. Likewise, early retirement programs — the "painless" approach to layoffs — are guaranteed to drive off veterans with organizational memory while retaining the newbies who have none.

The Baby Bells experienced this and then overextended the few employees remaining who understood their complex, interlinking systems.

- *Boomerang employment.*

  When the goal is to reduce headcount, not to reduce labor costs, employees leave by the front door and return through the back as contractors, doing the work that never went away. Presto! A $70,000 expense suddenly becomes a $150,000 one. What a deal!

- *Scrambled workflows.*

  Poorly planned layoffs are like the random removal of engine parts: You get a whole lot of clang for the buck. Some layoffs disrupt the horizontal flow of work as employees juggle responsibilities to cover missing players. Sometimes the vertical flow becomes dysfunctional. Look for this when downsizing eliminates an entire layer of management. It might be the right layer to remove, and then again, it might not.

  Overlayered organizations are amazingly adept at removing the wrong layer, usually one lower in the organization that was actually adding value.

More than sixty years of research has shown there is a right number of reporting layers for any given organization and a right level of work to be performed at each layer. Executives who don't understand this, at least intuitively, can easily hobble an already struggling organization.

To take any of the wrong approaches to restructuring is like achieving weight loss by chopping off an arm and a leg. The scales show the right number, but you'll never get the functionality you want.

There are two right ways to approach labor-cost reduction.

1 *Match the workers to the work.*

   Do this if you have had a drop in workload — fewer calls to the call center, fewer customers in the stores, fewer insurance policies to underwrite.

   Instead of just guessing how many positions to cut, first quantify the work that has to be done. You will need to observe, interview, and collect data. (Warning: Official-looking Excel spreadsheets with a lot of managers' guesses don't count as data.)

2 *Play junior industrial engineer.*

   Determine how much work one effective employee can do, and with simple arithmetic you can see how many people you really need. In two or three days of careful analysis, you'll arrive at a number that optimizes savings without damaging productivity or customer service.

   Better yet, design an improved work process and staff to support it. Begin by mapping your work processes, step by step, handoff by handoff. Talk to the people who do the work, not their bosses.

   Figure out how much time each element takes and what it costs the company. Then design a process that eliminates, combines, or shortens work elements.

> Often, wasteful work becomes obvious — checkers checking checkers and other redundancies, rework, lousy communication, fumbled handoffs and dropped cross-functional passes. All are costly.

Improved work design should take weeks, not months. Don't make it a science project. With a little focused effort, even amateurs using this approach can achieve a 10 percent to 15 percent payroll savings, and specialists in process redesign will do twice as well. If the difference between the old work design and the new one doesn't net enough savings, prioritize the remaining work and decide which of it has to go. Don't lapse into denial, hoping that somehow it'll all get done.

Be ruthless in slashing work that you simply don't have enough employees to do. Otherwise employees will decide for themselves which work to do and which to avoid. You're better off making those decisions yourself.

THE POINT

Don't let the tail wag the dog. If you must reduce labor costs, let the work drive the reductions. If you understand how much work there is to do, and have designed smarter work processes, then reduced staffing will leave you with a company that still functions. And with a little luck, it will function even better than before.

Acknowledgments

Our editor, Kim Long, is as close to a Renaissance man as we know. His guidance on all aspects of writing and publishing saved us. (If you think the "Renaissance" claim is over the top, then Google his publication list!) And thanks to Gregory McNamee for his contributions to the editing phase.

Our family has supported our efforts — including "the book" — with kind patience as we filled too many days and nights with work.

Linda Thaut, our comptroller (and much more), has a knack for getting things right. Her support on this book made it possible; we are grateful for that and much more.

Our team at Executive Leadership Group, Inc. provided their continuous intellectual support and occasional kick in the pants.

Denver Business Journal and their parent company, American City Business Journals, kindly permitted us to use material we had produced for them in a column we wrote. We are especially appreciative for the thoughtful guidance we've received over the years from DBJ's Neal Westergaard, Bruce Goldberg, and Bob Mook.

Dr. Al Bernstein, serial author and organizational wise man (sometimes wise guy) gave us feedback that was as unflinching as it was useful. He knows whereof he speaks.

Michael Anderson, British-Canadian management guru, has over the years been the sanity check for our ideas, the best of which he formed years before we did.

Rebecca Zweig knows about the business of business books, and works with the big names of that field; in her off time she coached us well and with angelic forbearance.

Dr. Milton Bennett is perhaps the preeminent expert on intercultural communication in the world. He has been a good friend, colleague, and stimulant to productive thinking. The chapter on how to develop good judgment describes his elegant formula.

David Mercer, Rear Admiral, US Navy (ret) repeatedly admonished us to "keep it simple, keep it simple, keep it simple." That advice was as required as he thought it was.

Dr. Elliott Jaques, who passed away several years ago, was an intellectual inspiration and a fantastic coach. He showed that the logic of management and leadership does not have to be a muddle — and his 50+ years of research prove it. Thank you, sir, wherever you are.

Kind words from Jon Greenert, Admiral, US Navy, kept us going more than he realizes.

Sometimes we quote or allude to leaders who have taught us something important. Sometimes we don't even allude to anyone; we just state something as though we figured it out on our own. We didn't. Among the teachers who have contributed our thinking reflected here are: are Dave Laube, former CIO of Qwest Communications; Brenda Davis, Global CIO global CIO for Molson Coors; Bryan Monkhouse, former COO of Irving Oil; Jan Frank, CEO/President at Pacific Compensation Insurance; Pete Daly, Vice Admiral, US Navy, (ret.), CEO, US Naval Institute; John Harvey, Admiral, US Navy (ret.); and John Richardson, Admiral, US Navy.

For those contributors and supporters we shamefully forgot to mention: we owe each of them a beer, which is more than anybody else mentioned here is likely to get.

Index

Made in the USA
Coppell, TX
28 April 2021

54666774R10089